A Moti Mahal Cookbook

On the
Kebab Trail

A Moti Mahal Cookbook

On the
Kebab Trail

MONISH GUJRAL

PENGUIN BOOKS

An imprint of Penguin Random House

PENGUIN BOOKS

USA | Canada | UK | Ireland | Australia
New Zealand | India | South Africa | China | Singapore

Penguin Books is part of the Penguin Random House group of companies
whose addresses can be found at global.penguinrandomhouse.com

Published by Penguin Random House India Pvt. Ltd
4th Floor, Capital Tower 1, MG Road,
Gurugram 122 002, Haryana, India

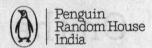

First published by Penguin Books India 2013

Copyright © Monish Gujral 2013

Foreword copyright © Vir Sanghvi 2013

10 9 8 7 6 5 4 3 2

ISBN 9780143419389

For sale in the Indian Subcontinent only

Typeset in Myriad Pro by Eleven Arts, Delhi

Printed at Repro India Limited

www.penguin.co.in

MIX
Paper from
responsible sources
FSC® C047271

To Maya (1875–1981)
Her eternal blessings always enrich our lives

Contents

Acknowledgements   viii
Foreword   ix
Introduction   xii

Basic Recipes and Spice Blends   1

Accompaniments   9

Kebabs   37
   Meat 39
   Poultry 116
   Seafood 187
   Vegetable 227

Glossary   275
Index   280
Author Note   287

Acknowledgements

The kebab has taken me through a long, global trail on which I have met some interesting people and gifted chefs. I thank all of them for contributing to my knowledge and experience—without that, this book would have been impossible to write.

To the gourmand family headed by Mr Edouard Cointreau, who in his own way has contributed to the world of culinary books, showcasing and recognizing the best in the world at the Paris Cookbook Fair, year after year.

My dear friend Vir Sangvi, for writing a beautiful foreword for this book, adding so much value to my work.

K.C. Walberg, a restaurateur–chef, who hosted me in Stockholm during one of my kebab trail expeditions. I have fond memories of experimenting with elk kebabs in his kitchen in Skansen, Stockholm.

Last, but not the least, to all my gurus, for their eternal blessings.

Foreword

Whenever you ask foreigners to name one Indian dish that they are familiar with, they tend to mention tandoori chicken. Or they name one of the famous chicken's derivatives: chicken tikka, butter chicken, chicken tikka masala.

When you inform them that these are not dishes that Indians cook at home, they look mystified. It takes a while to explain that most Indians—even north Indians—no longer keep tandoors in their gardens. (Or have large gardens, for that matter.) And that even when people did have tandoors in their courtyards, they were usually used for bread, not as a key step on the journey to butter chicken.

But the surprises continue. Because India is an ancient civilization, people assume that Indian food is as ancient as the Vedas or the Upanishads. When you tell them that most Indian food can be dated to the mediaeval rather than the ancient era, they are astonished. But their bemusement is greatest when you explain that tandoori chicken is not even a mediaeval dish. It was invented in the twentieth century and found fame after the 1950s. Moreover, this fame can be traced to a single restaurant.

There will always be disputes and counter-claims about the exact moment when tandoori chicken was created. And there will always be arguments about the exact location where this invention occurred: was it Lahore or Peshawar or Delhi?

But some things are clear. Contrary to the hype that sometimes envelops tandoori cuisine, this is not the food of the Afghans. The mujahidin do not roam the mountains, Kalashnikov in one hand and tandoori skewer in the other. This is, in fact, a very Indian style of cooking and its greatest proponents were not Afghans, Mughals or hardy Khazakh tribesmen. Tandoori cuisine is Punjab's gift to the world.

No restaurant did more for Indian cuisine in the twentieth century than Moti Mahal. The restaurant's celebrated founder Kundan Lal Gujral was the man who put tandoori chicken on the map. It was his cooks who pierced chickens with skewers, placed them in the tandoor and popularized the dish that we so love today. It was Gujral and his Moti Mahal cooks who invented butter chicken as a way of making use of unsold tandoori chickens or offering a gravy dish to Moti Mahal's customers. And it was Gujral who created the famous black dal of north Indian cuisine by adding a variation of his makhni sauce (used in butter chicken) to the dal that Punjabis ate at home.

As his grandson, Monish Gujral has a lot to live up to. Though Moti Mahal will always be associated with tandoori chicken, it is neither possible nor desirable to patent a great dish. And so, by the 1960s, restaurants across India were serving tandoori chicken. In the 1970s, the tandoori chicken flew to London where its younger sister, the chicken tikka, took residence in the British imagination and eventually became part of chicken tikka masala, the most popular Indian dish in Britain.

The challenge before Monish has been to retain Moti Mahal's primacy after so many decades of global competition and transmutation. To his credit, he has done a magnificent job of keeping Kundan Lal Gujral's memory alive. His Moti Mahal deluxe chain builds on the original Moti Mahal's menu while moving subtly with the times and offering meals in locations that are better appointed than the first Moti Mahal in Delhi's Daryaganj.

In recent years, Monish Gujral has become a missionary for the Moti Mahal legacy, demonstrating his dishes all over the world and launching a successful range of packaged foods based on the original Moti Mahal recipes.

At a time when Indian cuisine is in ferment, these are encouraging developments. First of all, one of our problems is that family culinary traditions are being broken because sons and grandsons refuse to follow in the footsteps of their fathers and grandfathers. Monish is that happy exception to this rule.

And secondly, one of Indian cuisine's weaknesses is that it relies on an oral tradition. Recipes are handed down from father to son, from cook to successor. Monish's books represent a break with this tradition and seek to record recipes and techniques that would otherwise be lost to posterity.

In the high-tech world of the twenty-first century, there is something reassuring and refreshing about a man taking his grandfather's legacy to every corner of the world because he knows that Moti Mahal is in his blood and great food is his destiny.

Vir Sanghvi

Introduction

Over the past few years, I have been on a kebab trail, travelling through the kingdoms of the kebab, from Turkey (which popularized the kebab) to the Middle East, and of course across India. In my travels I have hunted for the most unusual recipes, their histories and traditions, and this book is the fruit of my travels. I was born in a family of restaurateurs and chefs and run one of the most renowned restaurant chains in India. My grandfather created the tandoori chicken and the famous butter chicken, thus revolutionizing Indian cuisine and the plebeian village tandoor. So my passion for kebabs feels natural, a part of my heritage.

Strictly speaking, kebabs refers to small cuts of meat which are usually marinated and then grilled or roasted although in this book you will find vegetarian kebabs and examples of dishes where the meat has been fried. There are also countless varieties of kebabs across the world and it is worth remembering that it is eaten across Central and East Asia, the Middle East, South East Asia and even in some African countries. I have tried to include recipes from all these places.

There are several views about the origin of the word kebab. It may have been derived from the Arabic word *kab*, which means a turning movement and *cabob*, meaning a piece of meat, fish, poultry or vegetable, so that the fusion of these two words led to kebab. The Arabic word possibly derives from the Aramaic, *kabbābā*, which probably has its origins in *kabābu*—meaning 'to burn or char'.

Whatever the etymology, the kebab was most likely created as a result of a short supply of cooking fuel in the Near East. This made the cooking of large pieces of food difficult. Arabian tradition has it that the dish was created by mediaeval Turkish soldiers who used their swords to grill meat over open-field fires. In India, Ibn Batuta records that kebabs were served in royal houses from at least the mediaeval Sultanate period, and even commoners would enjoy it with naan for breakfast.

The dish though was most likely native to the Near East and ancient Greece. Excavations in Akrotiri on the Greek island of Santorini by Professor C.G. Doumas unearthed sets of stone barbecue skewers used before the seventeenth century BCE. Initially, the kebab was probably just a chunk of freshly killed animal meat smoked or cooked over a simple wooden fire with a little salt and perhaps some local herbs added to it. The subtle addition of flavours, textures and tastes was an art form that evolved over time.

The kebab may have had a long global history—from the wide array of Turkish kebabs, an essential part of Turkish cuisine which is a rich heritage of the Ottoman empire with influences from the Middle East, to Iranian kebabs and Central Asian kebabs such as Yangrouchan, the most popular dish in China, made up of chunks of mutton marinated with cumin and chilli paste and then threaded on bamboo showers and grilled on coal—but it reached its heights in India. You may call me biased, but it is only in this country that the grilled meat was combined with a genuinely sophisticated and innovative spice and condiment mix that turned this humble food into a delicacy. This sophistication came with the Mughals who bought with them exotic ingredients such as rose water, vetiver (or kewra), dried fruits, musk and poppy seeds.

As an aside, it's worth noting that the kebab had been popular in India before the Mughals. I have made a reference to Ibn Batuta earlier but the Rajputs also made *sulé* or smoked kebabs long before the Mughal invasion. Hunting was a popular sport of the maharajas and game meat was their favourite. It was often cooked over an open fire in the forests. All the meat was not consumed at one time, and was pickled to preserve it for the next day. The state of Palanpur (today on the border of Gujarat and Rajasthan) in particular was renowned for its kebabs. But it really was after the Mughal invasion that the dish was transformed.

Today many of India's states boast their own rich repertoire of kebabs. In Kashmir, kebabs are characterized by the use of delicate flavours such as cardamom, saffron, yogurt and aniseed. Kashmiri tabak maaz, a kebab of tender lamb rib, is a particular favourite of mine. Hyderabad is famous for its fiery food and its kebabs make use of the hot spices of Andhra Pradesh, unlike the Awadhi cuisine's galouti, kakori and shikampur kebabs which are so delicate that they melt in the mouth. Each region is utterly unique with its own special flavours and techniques.

While we have inherited many of these traditional recipes (many of which have been reproduced here), there is one distinct difference between the way we made kebabs in the past and the way we make them today. Kebabs were traditionally cooked on an open spit fire. Today they are largely cooked in tandoors or ovens and grills. The tandoor is a clay oven which was installed in the village centre and was called sanjha chulha. The village women would collect around it in the evenings with their dough and bake their bread. It originally came to India from Central Asia.

It was my grandfather Kundan Lal Gujral who transformed this plebeian village tandoor, using it in restaurants to make the tandoori chicken. As the story goes, young Kundan was asked by his mentor one day in the early 1900s to make a light chicken dish. Suddenly he thought of the novel idea of marinating the chicken with curd and some spices and finally grilling it. Since skewers weren't available easily, he used an iron wire to pierce the chicken and lowered it into the tandoor. What came out was the Tandoori Chicken. With this he made history or should I say that he initiated a new method of cooking—tandoori cuisine. And today we cook most kebabs in this fashion.

As you would have sensed by now, the delicious, succulent, exquisitely spiced kebabs that you love have had a long journey and many incarnations. The following pages will give you an even richer sense of their diversity and history and my ideas for fresh new variations. I hope you enjoy the journey.

Points to Remember While Making Kebabs

- Kebabs should not be over-cooked as they tend to dry up and get tough.
- Never reheat kebabs in a microwave oven as it makes them dry and leathery.
- When yogurt is used for the marinade it should be hung in a muslin cloth for about 30 minutes before use to drain off the excess whey.
- Marinades should be thick pastes, not runny liquids.

Cooking in a Tandoor Oven

- Temperature plays an important role in tandoori cooking; the charcoal should be evenly placed at the bottom of a tandoor if you are using a wood-fired one.
- The food being cooked is plunged into the tandoor where the temperature is about 600°C, whereby the outer portion of the food is cooked immediately, to form a seal. This preserves the juices of the food inside the food, where the temperature would be around 160°C.
- For tandoori cooking, basting is significant. It is the application of fat on the food being cooked which seals the juices and makes the kebabs succulent.
- Thread the food to be cooked on to skewers, 1 inch apart, and place them in a preheated, medium-hot tandoor for the time mentioned in the recipe.
- Remove the skewers and baste as given in the recipe, invert the skewers into the tandoor, to ensure even heating, and cook again for the time mentioned.

Grilling over a Charcoal Fire

- Thread the food on to skewers as explained above and place them over a charcoal fire that is glowing.

- Cook the food for the time mentioned in the recipe, turning the skewers and basting the food periodically.

Grilling over a Regular Gas or Electric Grill
- Thread the food on to skewers as explained above and arrange them on a lightly greased grill rack placed over a grill pan, to collect the drippings. Individual items can also be put directly on the rack.
- Preheat the grill to medium hot (200°C–220°C), hot (220°C–230°C) or very hot (240°C–250°C), according to the instructions in the recipe.
- Place the grill pan under the grill for the time specified.
- Remove the pan from the grill and baste the food. Turn the skewers or individual food items around and grill further, for the time specified in the recipe.

TABLE OF MEASURES

1 cup = 225 ml

1 tsp = 5 ml

1 tbsp = 3 tsp

A pinch = 1/8 tsp (literally a pinch)

A dash = 1–2 drops

BASIC RECIPES AND SPICE BLENDS

GINGER PASTE

Ginger 250 gm

- Wash the ginger well and soak in water overnight to soften the skin.
- Drain the ginger, peel and chop it roughly.
- Process in a grinder, till puréed, using very little water, if required.
- The paste can be stored in an airtight container and refrigerated for 4–6 weeks.

GARLIC PASTE

Garlic 250 gm

- Soak the garlic in water overnight to soften the skin.
- Drain the garlic, peel and chop it roughly.
- Process in a grinder, till puréed, using very little water, if required.
- The paste can be stored in an airtight container and refrigerated for 4–6 weeks.

ONION PASTE

Onion 500 gm

- Peel the onions and chop roughly.
- Process in a grinder, till puréed.

- The paste can be stored in an airtight container and refrigerated for 4–6 weeks.

BROWN ONION PASTE

Makes 200 gm

Oil 3 tbsp
Onions, medium-sized, sliced fine 4
Yogurt ½ cup

- Heat the oil in a heavy-bottomed, non-stick pan.
- Sauté the onions on high heat for about 5 minutes, till they turn translucent.
- Reduce heat to medium-low and continue sautéing for another 15 minutes, till it is caramelized and brown.
- Remove from heat and cool.
- Transfer to a grinder, add the yogurt and grind to make a smooth paste.
- Store in the refrigerator, till required.

TOMATO PURÉE

Makes 1½ cups

Tomatoes 1 kg
Oil 2 tsp
Salt 1 tsp

- Wash the tomatoes and chop them roughly.
- Heat the oil in a pan. Add the tomatoes and salt. Cook on medium heat, till tender and watery.

- Remove from heat and press through a strainer into a bowl. Discard the residue in the strainer.
- Store in the refrigerator and use as required.

COTTAGE CHEESE
PANEER

Makes 200 gm

Milk 1 litre
White vinegar 2 tbsp

- Bring the milk to a boil on high heat.
- Remove from heat, cool for a minute and add the vinegar.
- Stir gently, till the milk splits completely.
- Pour the contents of the pan into a strainer lined with muslin cloth and placed over a bowl.
- Press lightly to remove as much liquid as possible.
- Knead the residue to make a fine smooth dough.
- Store in the refrigerator, till required.

HUNG YOGURT

Makes 1 cup

Yogurt 3 cups

- Hang the yogurt in a muslin bag for 2 hours to drain, with a bowl underneath to catch the whey.
- Scoop out the drained yogurt from the muslin cloth and transfer to a bowl.
- Store in the refrigerator, till required.

CASHEW NUT AND CHEESE PASTE

Makes 2 tbsp

Cashew nuts 2½ tbsp
Processed Cheddar cheese, grated 2 tbsp
Milk ¼ cup
Cream, fresh, whisked 2 tbsp

- Grind all the ingredients to a smooth paste.
- Use as required.

AROMATIC SPICE MASALA POWDER

Makes 500 gm

Mace flakes 250 gm
Green cardamoms 250 gm

- Put the ingredients in a grinder and grind to make a fine powder.
- Sift and store in an airtight container.

GARAM MASALA POWDER

Makes about 750 gm

Cumin seeds 200 gm
Whole black pepper 350 gm

Green cardamoms 2½ tbsp
Black cardamoms 11
Coriander seeds 12 tbsp
Cloves 4 tbsp
Cinnamon 20 x 1" sticks
Mace powder 2 tbsp
Bay leaves 7
Ginger, dried, powdered 6 tbsp
Nutmeg, roughly smashed 2

- Roast each ingredient separately in a dry pan on medium heat, till aromatic.
- Remove from heat and set aside, till cool.
- Put all the ingredients in a grinder and grind to make a fine powder.
- Sift and store in an airtight container.

TANDOORI MASALA POWDER

Makes 1¾ kg

Coriander seeds 400 gm
Cumin seeds 400 gm
Black cumin seeds 100 gm
Rose petals, dried 250 gm
Mace flakes 150 gm
Cinnamon sticks 150 gm
Whole black pepper 100 gm
Star anise 60 gm
Green cardamoms 30 gm
Black cardamoms 50 gm
Cloves 30 gm
Nutmeg 30 gm

- Clean all the ingredients and place them under a high-voltage bulb or in the sun, covered with a fine muslin cloth for 1–2 hours, to dry out slightly.
- Put all the ingredients in a grinder and grind to make a fine powder.
- Sift and store in an airtight container.

MIDDLE EASTERN SPICE BLEND
ZHOUG

Makes 8 tbsp

Jalapeno peppers, seeded, chopped coarsely 4
Pumpkin seeds, toasted, shelled 1 tsp
Coriander leaves, fresh, with tender stems 4 tbsp
Parsley, fresh 2 tbsp
Garlic ½ a clove
Coriander powder a pinch
Cumin powder a pinch
Olive oil, extra virgin 1 tsp
Rice vinegar a few drops
Salt to taste
Black pepper, freshly ground to taste

- Grind all the ingredients, except the salt and pepper, to make a smooth paste.
- Taste and add salt and pepper.

ACCOMPANIMENTS

CHUTNEYS

～

CHILLI GARLIC CHUTNEY
LASSUN MIRCH CHUTNEY

Makes ½ cup

Red chillies, dried, kept whole 40 gm
Garlic paste 2 tbsp
Lime juice 1½ tbsp
Oil 1 tbsp
Salt 1 tsp

- Soak the red chillies in hot water for about 30 minutes.
- Drain and put them in a grinder with the remaining ingredients.
- Grind to make a semi-smooth paste, adding a little water if required.
- Set aside to mature for 2–3 hours before use.

CORIANDER CHUTNEY
DHANIA CHUTNEY

Makes about 1¼ cups

Coriander leaves, fresh, chopped 1 cup
Mint leaves, fresh, chopped 3 tbsp
Green chillies, seeded, chopped 6
Ginger, chopped 2 tbsp

Lime juice 1 lime
Cumin seeds, pounded ½ tsp
Salt 1 tsp

- Wash the coriander and mint leaves thoroughly and drain well.
- Combine all the ingredients in a grinder and blend to make a smooth paste. Sprinkle in a little water, if required.
- Transfer to a serving bowl and place in the refrigerator, till required.

MINT CHUTNEY
PUDINA CHUTNEY

This is the famous Moti Mahal chutney.

Makes 2 ¼ cups

Mint leaves, fresh, chopped 2 cups
Coriander leaves, fresh, chopped 2 cups
Green chillies, seeded, chopped fine 16
Ginger, chopped fine 2 tbsp
Yogurt 1 cup
Pomegranate seeds, dried 3 tbsp
Salt 2 tsp
Lime juice 1 lime

- Wash the mint and coriander leaves thoroughly and drain well.
- Combine all the ingredients, except the salt and lime juice, in a grinder and blend to make a smooth paste.
- Add the salt and lime juice and blend once more.
- Transfer to a serving bowl and place in the refrigerator, till required.

MANGO CHUTNEY

AAM KI CHUTNEY

Makes 1 kg

Mangoes, raw, green 1½ kg
Onions, grated 1 cup
Ginger paste 3½ tbsp
Garlic paste 1½ tbsp
Raisins, seedless 100 gm
Melon seeds 1 tbsp
Sugar 1 kg
Red chilli powder 1 tbsp
Garam masala powder 1 tbsp
Cinnamon powder ½ tsp
White vinegar 1 cup
Salt 3 tsp

- Wash the mangoes and peel them. Chop the flesh and discard the stones. Set aside.
- Combine the onions and ginger paste in a muslin cloth and squeeze out as much juice as possible.
- Mix the onion and ginger juice with the garlic paste and set aside in a bowl. Discard the residue in the muslin.
- Soak the raisins and melon seed in a bowl of water for 30 minutes. Drain and dry in paper towels. Set aside.
- Put the mangoes and sugar in a heavy-bottomed pan on medium heat and cook for 12–15 minutes, stirring occasionally.
- Add the onion–ginger–garlic paste and spice powders and simmer on medium heat, stirring frequently, till it has a jam-like consistency.
- Mix in the vinegar and salt and cook for 2–3 minutes longer.
- Remove from heat and stir in the dried raisins and melon seeds.
- Cool and transfer to an airtight jar.
- Set aside to mature for 2–3 days before use.

SESAME TOMATO CHUTNEY

TIL AUR TAMATAR KI CHUTNEY

Makes ½ cup

Groundnut oil 2 tbsp
Onions, chopped 1 cup
Red chilli powder ½ tsp
Turmeric powder ½ tsp
Asafoetida powder a pinch
Sesame seeds 2 tbsp
Tomatoes, chopped 1 cup
Husked, split black gram/urad dal, roasted 4 tsp

For tempering
Oil 1¼ tbsp
Red chillies, dried, kept whole 5
Curry leaves, fresh 2 sprigs
Mustard seeds ½ tsp

- Heat the oil in a pan. Add the onions and sauté on medium heat, till light brown.
- Stir in the spice powders and sesame seeds. Sauté for a few minutes longer, till aromatic.
- Add the tomatoes along with the gram and cook for about 10 minutes, stirring periodically.
- Remove from heat and set aside, till cool.
- Blend to make a coarse paste and pour into a bowl.
- Heat the oil for the tempering in a small pan. Add the tempering ingredients and sauté on medium heat, till they splutter.
- Pour the contents of the pan over the chutney and serve.

PEANUT CHUTNEY

Makes ½ cup

Peanuts, roasted, peeled ½ cup
Green chillies 2
Ginger, chopped 1 tsp
Garlic, chopped 3 cloves
Lime juice 2 tbsp
Groundnut oil 1 tbsp
Salt 1 tsp

- Put all the ingredients in a blender and grind to make a paste slightly granular in consistency. Add a little water if required.
- Transfer to a serving bowl and place in the refrigerator, till required.

HOT CHILLI SAUCE

Makes ½ cup

Red chillies, dried 10
Garlic 3 cloves
Salt 2 tbsp
White vinegar ½ cup
Sherry 1 tbsp

- Remove the stems of the red chillies and discard.
- Place the chillies in a small bowl and pour enough boiling water to cover them.
- Put a small plate over the chillies, so that they are totally submerged.
- Set aside for 20 minutes.
- Drain the chillies and grind with the garlic, salt and vinegar, to make a smooth paste.
- Add ½ cup of water and grind again, to give the sauce a pouring consistency.
- Blend in the sherry.

HOT SATAY PEANUT SAUCE

Makes about 500 ml

Garlic 3 cloves
Spanish onions, medium-sized, chopped roughly 2
Macadamia nuts 8
Lemon grass, white part only, chopped 2 stalks
Oil 1 tbsp

Mixed Malaysian curry powder, commercial 1½ tbsp
Tamarind paste 1 ½ tbsp
Sambal oelek 2 tsp
Peanuts, unsalted, roasted 150 gm
Or **crunchy peanut butter 125 gm**
Coconut milk 350 ml
Sugar to taste
Salt to taste

- Blend the garlic, onions, macadamia nuts and lemon grass together to make a smooth paste.
- Heat the oil in a pan. Add the paste and sauté on medium to high heat, for 3–5 minutes, till it is caramelized. Stir continuously and add a little extra oil, if necessary, to prevent the mixture from sticking to the bottom of the pan.
- Add the curry powder, tamarind paste and sambal oelek. Stir well and fry on medium heat for a few minutes.
- Mix in the peanuts or peanut butter, coconut milk and 1 cup of hot water.
- Simmer, stirring all the while, till the sauce has a pouring consistency. (The sauce reduces rapidly, so stir it continuously.)
- If the sauce is too thick, add some more hot water and stir well.
- Taste and add sugar and salt.
- For a spicier peanut sauce, add more sambal oelek.

TERIYAKI SAUCE

Teriyaki sauce is available in the market, but it's easily made at home. Just follow my simple recipe.

Makes ½ cup

Ginger, grated ¼ tbsp
Brown sugar ¾ tbsp

Garlic, minced ¼ clove
Soy sauce 1 tbsp
Cornflour ½ tbsp

- Combine all the ingredients, except the cornflour, in a small pan on medium heat.
- Add 1 tbsp of water and bring to a boil, stirring constantly.
- Slake the cornflour in 1 tbsp of cold water and add it to the sauce.
- Stir continuously, till the sauce thickens.
- If it gets too thick, add a little water or soy sauce.

RAITAS AND SALADS

CUCUMBER AND YOGURT RELISH

IRANI RAITA

Makes 4 cups

Cucumbers 450 gm
Yogurt, whisked 4 cups
Honey 5 tbsp
Raisins, seedless, chopped 3 tbsp
White pepper powder, freshly ground ½ tsp
Salt 1 tsp
Cumin seeds, roasted, powdered ½ tsp
Coriander leaves, fresh, chopped 1 tsp

- Peel the cucumbers and chop them fine.
- Put the yogurt in a bowl and mix in the remaining ingredients.
- Chill and serve sprinkled with coriander leaves.

CUMIN AND YOGURT RELISH

JEERA RAITA

Makes 2 cups

Cumin seeds 1 tsp
Yoghurt 2 cups
Salt 1½ tsp
Cumin powder ½ tsp

Coriander leaves fresh, chopped 1 tsp

- Roast the cumin seeds in a dry pan on medium heat till golden-brown and fragrant. Set aside till cool and transfer to a bowl.
- Add the cumin powder, salt and yogurt and whisk, till well blended.
- Sprinkle coriander leaves on top and refrigerate till chilled.

SPINACH AND YOGURT RELISH

PALAK RAITA

Makes 2 cups

Spinach, tender leaves, whole 15
Olive oil 2 tsp
Dried red chillies, whole 2
Mustard seeds ½ tsp
Salt 2 tsp
Yogurt 2 cups

- Remove the stems of the spinach leaves and discard. Keep the leaves whole.
- Blanch the spinach leaves in hot water for 3–4 minutes and drain thoroughly.
- Put the oil in a pan on medium heat. When hot, add the red chillies and mustard seed and sauté, till they splutter
- Add the salt and spinach and sauté for 2 minutes.
- Transfer the contents of the pan to a bowl and set aside, till it reaches room temperature.
- Whisk the curd and pour it over the spinach. Mix well.
- Refrigerate and serve chilled.

BEETROOT AND
POMEGRANATE RELISH

CHUKUNDAR AUR ANAR RAITA

Makes 2 cups

Beetroot, medium-sized 1
Yoghurt 2 cups
Pomegranate seeds, fresh 2 tbsp
Salt 1 tsp
Mint leaves, fresh, chopped 2 tbsp

- Scrub the beetroot and boil it till tender. Peel and grate it.
- Whisk the yogurt in a bowl and add the beetroot, pomegranate seeds and salt. Mix well till the yogurt turns red.
- Serve chilled sprinkled with mint leaves.

GREEK SALAD

Makes 2–3

Greek salad is a rough, country salad of tomato, cucumber, red onion, green pepper, crumbly feta cheese and kalamata olives. It can be served as a side dish or as a light meal with some crusty bread.

For the salad
Tomatoes, cut into wedges 3
Red onion, sliced in rings ¼
Cucumber, sliced into thick half-rounds ½
Green bell pepper, cut in juliennes ½

Feta cheese, cut into small cubes 100 gm
Kalamata olives 12
Black pepper, freshly ground to taste

For the dressing
Garlic, minced 1 clove
Oregano, dried ½ tsp
Sea salt ¼ tsp
Black pepper, freshly ground ½ tsp
Olive oil, extra virgin 4 tbsp
Lime juice 1 tbsp

- Combine the dressing ingredients in a small jar with a screw-top lid and shake to blend. Put the salad ingredients in a large bowl.
- Pour the dressing over the salad and toss gently to coat, just before serving.
- Grind a little black pepper on top and serve.

VARIATIONS:
Blanch the onions, if you prefer a milder flavour.
  Instead of feta cheese, use thickly sliced haloumi cheese, lightly fried on both sides till golden. Use only olive oil, salt and pepper for the dressing and sprinkle fresh basil leaves on top.

MOROCCAN COUSCOUS SALAD

Makes 4

For the couscous
Olive oil 1 tbsp
Turmeric powder ¼ tsp
Cinnamon powder ¼ tsp

Ginger, dried, powder ¼ tsp
Paprika ¼ tsp
Cumin seeds ¼ tsp
Couscous 2 cups

For the dressing
Brown sugar 1–2 tbsp
Salt 1½ tsp
Olive oil 3 tbsp
Orange juice ¼ cup

For the salad
Chickpeas, cooked 400 gm
Oranges, peeled, pith and seeds removed 200 gm
Red onion, chopped 1
Bell pepper, green or red, chopped 1
Raisins, seedless ¼ cup

For the garnish
Coriander leaves, fresh, chopped 2–3 tbsp
Almonds 2 tbsp (optional)

- Heat 1 tbsp of oil in a pan. Add the spice powders, cumin seeds and couscous. Stir for 2–3 minutes on medium heat, till fragrant. Toss continuously, to prevent burning.
- Add 2½ cups of water and bring to a boil.
- Reduce heat to low, cover the pan and simmer for 5 minutes, till all the liquid is absorbed. Remove from heat and set aside for 5–10 minutes.
- Transfer to serving bowl and stir gently.
- Put the dressing ingredients in a screw-top jar and shake, till well blended.
- Add the salad ingredients with the dressing to the couscous.
- Toss, till the ingredients are well distributed and coated with the dressing.
- Sprinkle the coriander leaves and almonds on top and serve at room temperature.

FLATBREADS

~∽~

I belong to an Indian Punjabi family where the tandoori roti or paratha (Indian flatbreads) is a must with every meal. For breakfast my granny made parathas stuffed with spicy potato or a cottage cheese and coriander mix, or even unripe papaya grated and mixed with a spice blend, oozing with ghee and cooked to perfection. Lunch, of course, was generally served with crisp tandoori rotis, vegetables, chicken curry and home-made, creamy yoghurt. For me, there is no better meal than one accompanied by Indian flatbreads, kebabs and chutneys. However, I have recently found that our kebabs taste as good with breads from other countries. Here are some recipes for you to experiment with.

PITA BREAD

Makes 8

Pita is one of my favourite breads as it goes well with most kebabs and dips.

This recipe makes soft, white pita rounds that should be brushed with olive oil and grilled, heated in a skillet, or toasted in the oven before serving. Serve it cut in wedges with dips, as a wrap for sandwiches, and in other creative ways.

2 tsp yeast
Flour, refined 3 cups + extra for rolling
Salt 1¼ tsp
Honey or sugar 1 tsp
Butter or oil 2 tbsp
Water 1½ cups

- Dissolve the yeast in ½ cup of warm water. Add the sugar or honey and stir till it is dissolved. Set aside for 10–15 minutes, till frothy.
- Sift the flour with the salt into a large bowl.
- Make a well in the centre of the flour and pour in the yeast.
- Slowly add 1 cup of warm water, and stir with a wooden spoon or rubber spatula to make an elastic dough.
- Place the dough on a lightly floured surface and knead for 10–15 minutes, till the dough is smooth and no longer sticky.
- Shape into a ball and place it in a large bowl lightly greased with butter or oil.
- Rotate the dough ball in the bowl, so that it is coated with the butter or oil.
- Cover and set aside in a warm place for about 3 hours, or till it has doubled in size.
- Knead the dough again and roll it out into a rope. Cut it into 8 portions and shape into balls.
- Place them on a lightly floured surface, cover and set aside for 10 minutes. Preheat the oven to 250°C and ensure that the rack is at the very bottom of oven. Be sure to also preheat your baking sheet.
- Roll out each ball of dough into 5"–6" round discs, ¼" thick, and put on the preheated baking sheet.
- Bake each disc for 4 minutes, till the bread puffs up. Turn over and bake for 2 minutes longer.
- Remove the pita with a spatula from the baking sheet and enjoy your hot pitas with a choice of kebabs and chutneys.

NOTE:

Pita bread can be stored for up to a week in an airtight bread box at room temperature or a month in the freezer, packed in freezer bags.

Gently press down the puff with a spatula after removing it from the oven and cool completely before storing.

WHOLEWHEAT PITA BREAD COOKED ON THE STOVE TOP

Makes 8

Yeast, dried 1½ tsp
Honey or sugar 1 tsp
Flour, wholewheat 2 cups
Flour, refined 1 cup
Salt 1 tsp
Olive oil 1 tsp
Water 1½ cups

- Make the dough following the instructions given for pita bread (p. 24) and roll out 8 portions.
- Place a heavy-bottomed pan that has a tight lid on medium heat and brush with oil.
- Put a pita disc in the pan and cover it for 2–3 minutes.
- Open the pan and turn the bread over. Cover and cook for 2 minutes longer.
- Remove the bread from the pan and serve hot

ITALIAN FLATBREAD

Makes 8

Flour, refined 4 cups
Olive oil 1/3 cup
Baking soda 1 tsp
Salt ½ tsp
Sugar ¼ tsp
Milk 100 ml
Water 100 ml (½ cup and 1 tbsp)

- Blend all the ingredients with 100 ml of water in a food processor. Add more flour or water as required, to form a smooth and non-sticky dough.
- Set aside to rest for at least 2 hours.
- Divide the dough into 8 portions and shape into balls.
- Roll each ball on a lightly floured surface into 10" discs.
- Put a non-stick frying pan on medium-high heat. When hot, put a disc on the pan.
- Cook for 3-4 minutes, till the base is pale gold with dark brown spots. Flip over and cook the other side.
- Serve hot.

NORWEGIAN FLATBREAD

Makes 8

This is a simple, delicious cracker-like bread.

Flour, wholewheat 1 cup
Flour, refined 1 cup
Salt ½ tsp
Baking soda ¾ tsp
Sugar ¼ tsp
Oil ¼ cup
Buttermilk ¾ cup

- Preheat the oven to 175°C.
- Sift both the flours with the salt and baking soda into a bowl.
- Add the sugar and oil and mix well.
- Gradually add the buttermilk, mixing well till it forms a stiff, smooth dough.
- Knead the dough on a lightly floured work surface for a few minutes.
- Cover the dough with a damp cloth and set aside for 2–3 hours.

- Take ¼ cup of dough at a time and shape it into a ball. Pat it into a flat disc.
- Roll the dough into 10" round discs with a rolling pin on a lightly floured surface.
- Place the rolled dough on to un-greased baking sheets.
- Score the dough into 8 wedges by running a knife lightly across the discs, without cutting through to the other side.
- Bake in the preheated oven for 8–10 minutes.
- Remove and cool on wire racks.
- Break the discs along the scored lines.
- Top with butter or cheese and serve hot.

TORTILLAS

Makes 10

Flour, refined 3 cups + extra for rolling
Baking powder 2 tsp
Salt 2 tsp
Butter ¾ cup
Hot water ¾ cup

- Sift the flour, baking powder and salt into a bowl.
- Add the butter and mix with your fingertips, till it resembles breadcrumbs.
- If the mixture looks too dry, add 1–2 tbsp more butter and mix again.
- Gradually add up to ¾ cup of hot water and mix to make the ingredients moist.
- Knead, till the dough is smooth.
- If the dough still sticks to the side of the bowl, add 1–2 tbsp of flour and knead again.
- Cover with a damp cloth and set aside to rest for 3–4 hours.
- Divide the dough into 10 equal balls.

- Roll each ball on a lightly floured surface into a disc, about 1/8" thick.
- Cook each tortilla on a medium-hot cast-iron skillet for 1–2 minutes on each side.
- Serve hot.

TURKISH LAVASH

Makes 8

This is a thin Turkish flatbread.

Yeast, active, dry 2 tsp
Flour, refined 2½ cups + extra for rolling
Salt 1 tsp
Sugar ½ tsp
Olive oil, virgin 2 tbsp
Water 1¼ cups

- Dissolve the yeast in ½ cup of the lukewarm water and set aside for about 10 minutes, till frothy.
- Sift the flour and salt into a bowl.
- Mix in the sugar.
- Make a well in the centre and pour in the yeast with ¾ cup of lukewarm water.
- Mix with a wooden spatula to make a smooth dough.
- Knead the dough on a lightly floured surface, till smooth and pliable.
- Shape the dough into a ball and put it into a lightly greased bowl. Rotate the dough in the bowl, so that it is coated with oil.
- Cover with a damp cloth and set for 2 hours in a warm place to rise, till double in size.
- Transfer the dough to a lightly floured surface and knead again.

- Divide the dough into 8 equal portions.
- Flatten each portion with your hands or a rolling pin and shape into discs.
- Place a non-stick pan over medium heat. When hot, put the discs in the pan and brown both sides lightly.
- Serve immediately.

MOROCCAN FLATBREAD

Makes 4

For the dough
Yeast, active, dry ¼ tsp
Refined flour 1 cup
Salt ½ tsp
Sugar ¼ tsp

For the filling
Onion, medium, very finely chopped 1
Parsley, fresh, finely chopped ¼ cup
Butter, unsalted, softened 3 tbsp + 2 tbsp for greasing
Cumin powder ½ tsp
Paprika 1 tsp
Red pepper flakes, crushed ¼ tsp
Salt to taste

- Stir the yeast into ½ cup of lukewarm water and leave for 5–10 minutes, till frothy.
- Sift the flour and salt into a large bowl.
- Add the sugar. Pour in the yeast gradually and mix, till the dough is slightly moist. Knead the dough, till it is smooth and pliable. Set aside.
- Put all the filling ingredients in a mixing bowl, add salt to taste and blend together with your hands.

- Smear a work surface and your hands with extra butter and divide the dough into 4 equal portions.
- Flatten each portion with your fingers into a very thin square, stretching it carefully, ensuring it does not tear.
- Spread a quarter of the filling over one half of each square and fold the plain side over. Fold again to form small squares. Flatten as thin as possible with your fingers or use a rolling pin if necessary.
- Grease a large non-stick frying pan with a little butter and place it over medium-high heat.
- Put the folded dough squares in the pan and cook for 3–4 minutes on each side, till light gold all over.
- Remove and place on a wire rack.
- Serve hot or warm.

GARLIC FLATBREAD

Makes 2

Flour, wholewheat ¼ cup
1 cup warm water, divided
Yeast, dry ½ tsp
Flour, refined 2 cups + ¼ cup
Salt ½ tsp
Sugar ¼ tsp
Olive oil 1 tbsp
Cornmeal 1 tsp
Cooking spray as required
Garlic, finely sliced 4 cloves

- Combine the wholewheat flour, yeast and ¼ cup of water in a bowl. Whisk, till well blended. Set aside for 10 minutes.
- Combine 2 cups of refined flour with the salt, sugar and ¾ cup of water in another bowl. Mix, till well blended.

- Add the wholewheat flour and yeast mixture.
- Stir till the dough is smooth and non-sticky.
- Knead the dough on a lightly floured surface for about 10 minutes, till smooth and elastic.
- Add 1 tbsp of the remaining refined flour at a time, and continue to knead, till the dough no longer sticks to your hands.
- Shape the dough into a ball and put it into a bowl lightly greased with olive oil. Rotate the dough in the bowl, so that it is coated with oil.
- Cover with a damp cloth and set for 1 hour in a warm place to rise, till double in size.
- Preheat the oven to 230°C.
- Punch the dough down, cover and let it rest for 5 minutes.
- Divide the dough into half and shape into 2 balls.
- Roll each half into a 9" disc on a lightly floured surface.
- Place the discs on baking sheets sprinkled with cornmeal.
- Lightly coat dough with cooking spray.
- Sprinkle the tops evenly with garlic and press the garlic in gently with your fingertips.
- Bake in centre of the preheated oven for 10 minutes, till the bread is crisp and the garlic begins to brown.
- Remove and cool on wire racks.
- Serve hot.

ROSEMARY FLATBREAD

Makes 4

Flour, refined 1½ cups
Baking powder ¾ tsp
Salt ¾ tsp
Rosemary, fresh, chopped 1 tbsp

Honey or sugar ¼ tsp
Olive oil 1/3 cup + 2 tbsp
Sea salt 1½ tsp

- Preheat the oven to 200°C with a heavy baking sheet or a sheet of aluminium foil on the rack in the centre of the oven.
- Sift the flour, baking powder and salt into a bowl. Reserve a few leaves of rosemary and add the remaining to the bowl with the honey or sugar. Mix, till the ingredients are well distributed.
- Make a well in the centre.
- Whisk 1/3 cup of oil with ½ cup of water in a jug and gradually stir it into the flour with a wooden spatula, till the dough is smooth and elastic.
- Knead gently on a work surface for 3–4 minutes.
- Divide the dough into 4 balls and roll out each on a lightly floured surface into a 10" round disc.
- Lightly brush the top with extra oil and sprinkle the reserved rosemary leaves on top, pressing them in slightly. Sprinkle with sea salt.
- Place them on the preheated baking sheet or aluminium foil and bake for 8–10 minutes till pale gold.
- Transfer to a rack to cool.

NAAN

Makes 8

Flour, refined 4 cups
Baking powder ½ tsp
Salt 1 tsp
Sugar 1 tbsp
Egg, whisked 1

Milk ½ cup
Oil 4 tbsp
Nigella seeds 1 tsp

- Sift the flour, baking powder and salt into a bowl.
- Mix the sugar, egg, milk and 2 tbsp of oil in another bowl, till well blended.
- Make a well in the centre of the flour and pour in the milk mixture.
- Mix well and knead, adding a little water if required, to form a smooth, soft dough that is no longer sticky.
- Add the remaining oil and knead again.
- Cover with a damp cloth and set aside for 15–20 minutes.
- Knead the dough again, cover and set aside for 2–3 hours.
- About 30 minutes before cooking the naan, turn the oven on to its highest temperature.
- Divide the dough into 8 balls and allow to rest for 5 minutes.
- Shape each ball of dough with the palms of your hands to make an oval shape.
- Sprinkle nigella seeds on top and put it in the oven.
- Bake, till the naan is puffed up and golden-brown.
- Serve hot.

BUTTER FLATBREAD

MAKHAN ROTI

Makes 2

Makhan roti is made with wholewheat flour and can be eaten with any curry or kebab.

Flour, wholewheat 1½ cups
Cumin seeds 1 tsp
Sugar ¼ tsp

Salt ¼ tsp
Butter, melted ¼ cup + extra for rolling and cooking
¾ cup warm water

- Mix the flour, cumin seeds, sugar and salt in a bowl. Add ¾ cup of warm water and mix till well blended.
- Knead the dough, till it is smooth and no longer sticky.
- Cover the dough with a damp cloth and set aside for 1 hour.
- Add the melted butter to the dough and knead again.
- Divide the dough into lime-sized balls and press down gently to form a patty. Roll the patties into 8" discs.
- Put a tava or griddle on medium heat. When hot, put a roti on the tava. Lightly brush with melted butter. When the base is cooked, turn it over to cook the other side. Spread some more butter on top and cook, till both sides are light golden brown.
- Serve hot with a choice of kebab and curries.

KEBABS

MEAT

Mutton can be substituted
by lamb in all the recipes

SPICY MINCED MUTTON PATTIES

CHAPLI KEBAB

Makes 2

While I was growing up, I would laugh whenever I heard this name, as *chapli* means slippers in Hindi, and ask: 'Is this made with your rubber slippers?'

Nevertheless, chapli kebab, a mince patty generally served with naan, is a delicacy from Peshawar in Pakistan, popular even in Afghanistan at barbecues. Chapli is derived from the Pashto word *chaprikh* which means flat. The dish originates in Mardan (Takhtbhai) and Manshera (Qalanderabad) in Pakistan. My grandmother, who migrated from Peshawar to India during the Partition of 1947, often spoke about it.

Mutton, minced 200 gm
Salt 1 tsp
Green chillies, chopped fine 1 tsp
Onion paste 4 tsp (p. 3)
Coriander leaves, fresh, chopped fine 1 tsp
Lime juice 1 tsp
Maize flour 1 tbsp
Green cardamom powder ½ tsp
Cumin seeds 1 tsp
Coriander seeds 2 tsp
Pomegranate seeds, dried, crushed 1 tsp
Sodium bicarbonate ⅓ tsp
Oil for frying

- Put the mince in a bowl and add 1 tbsp of water to soften it.
- Add the remaining ingredients for the kebabs. Mix and rub it well with your palms.
- Set aside in the refrigerator for 3–4 hours.
- Remove the kebab mix from the refrigerator and bring to room temperature.
- Grease your hands lightly and divide the mix into two equal portions.
- Roll into balls and flatten them slightly to form round patties.
- Heat the oil in a non-stick frying pan and shallow-fry the kebabs, till golden-brown and crisp on both the sides.
- Drain on kitchen paper.
- Serve hot with naan (p. 33) and mint chutney (p. 12).

MINCED MUTTON PATTIES
KASHMIRI SHAMMI KEBAB

Makes 2–3

An excellent snack option, which I normally enjoy with Italian flatbread—an amazing fusion.

Mutton, boneless 250 gm
Husked, split Bengal gram/chana dal 2½ tbsp
Green cardamoms 4
Black cardamoms 2
Cinnamon 2 x 1" sticks
Red Kashmiri chilli powder ½ tsp
Ginger, dried, powdered ½ tsp
Garlic, chopped fine 2–3 cloves
Salt 1½ tsp
Green chillies, chopped fine ½ tsp
Coriander leaves, fresh, chopped fine 1 tbsp
Ginger, chopped fine 1 tsp
Black cumin seeds ½ tsp
Turmeric powder ½ tsp
Oil for deep-frying
Chaat masala powder 1 tsp
Onion, large, sliced 1

- Wash the meat, trim and drain. Cut it into large chunks.
- Put the meat into a pan with the gram, whole spices, spice powders, garlic and salt.
- Add just enough water to cover the contents of the pan and cook on low heat, till the water evaporates and the meat is tender
- Remove the pan from the heat and set aside till cool.
- Remove and discard the whole spices from the pan.
- Grind the kebab mix in a food processor, till it becomes a fine paste.

- Transfer the paste to a bowl and add the green chillies, coriander leaves, ginger, cumin seeds and turmeric powder. Mix well.
- Taste and add more salt, if required.
- Grease your hands lightly and divide the kebab mix into 4 equal portions. Roll each portion into balls and flatten them slightly to form round patties.
- Heat the oil in a frying pan. Deep-fry the kebabs on medium heat, till golden-brown and crisp on both sides.
- Drain on kitchen paper.
- Arrange the kebabs on a serving platter and sprinkle chaat masala powder on top. Serve hot with onion slices, mint chutney (p. 12) and Italian flatbread (p. 26).

SMOKED MUTTON PATTIES

KAKORI KEBAB

Makes 2

Kakori kebab is a South Asian kebab that originated in Kakori, a small hamlet on the outskirts of Lucknow in Uttar Pradesh, India. There is much folklore about this famous kebab. One story is that it was created by the Nawab of Kakori, Syed Mohammad Haider Kazmi, who was offended by a British officer's remark on the rough and coarse texture of the kebabs served at dinner. The Nawab ordered his rakabdars (royal gourmet cooks) to prepare a refined seekh kebab. After a brainstorming session which lasted for several days, they created a kebab so soft and juicy that it was applauded by the same officer.

The secret to this kebab lies in the ingredients used by the royal cooks: mince obtained from no other part but the raan ki machhli (tendon of the leg of mutton), and a mix of powdered aromatic spices.

Mutton, minced 200 gm
Papaya, unripe, paste 1 tbsp
Salt 1½ tsp
Garam masala powder ½ tsp
Yellow chilli powder ½ tsp
Gram flour, roasted 2 tsp
Brown onion paste 1 tsp (p. 4)
Poppy seed paste ½ tsp
Ginger–garlic paste ½ tsp
Nigella seed paste 1 tsp
Oil 1 tsp
Rose water 1 tsp
Charcoal, red-hot 1 piece
Cloves 3
Ghee ½ tsp
Oil for shallow-frying

Chaat masala powder 1 tsp
Coriander leaves, fresh, chopped 1 tbsp

For the mince

- Pass the mutton twice through the mincer to get a very fine mince.
- Place the mince in a large bowl with the papaya paste, salt, garam masala powder and chilli powder.
- Mix well, cover and set aside in the refrigerator for about 2 hours.
- Remove the meat from the refrigerator and bring to room temperature.

To smoke the kebab mix

- Make a well in the centre of the mince and place a small bowl in it.
- Put the red-hot charcoal piece in the small bowl.
- Add the cloves and ghee and cover the large bowl.
- Put a heavy weight on the lid, to seal it.
- Set aside for 3–4 minutes, to smoke the kebab mix.

For the kebabs

- Uncover the bowl and add the remaining ingredients for the kebabs. Mix well, till the ingredients are properly blended.
- Grease your hands lightly and roll the mix into small balls. Flatten them slightly to form round patties.
- Heat the oil in a non-stick frying pan and shallow-fry the kebabs in batches, if necessary, till golden brown and cooked through.
- Drain on kitchen paper.
- Arrange the kebabs on a serving platter and sprinkle chaat masala powder and coriander leaves on top. Serve hot with mint chutney (p. 12).

MINCED MUTTON STRIPS

DIGI KEBAB

Makes 2–3

I often cook these easy-to-make and no-fuss kebabs at home. Just mix all the ingredients together, let it rest for a while and put it under a grill. My kids enjoy it with naan, while watching TV.

Mutton, ground 500 gm
Onion, grated 1½
Green cardamom powder ½ tsp
Red chilli powder ½ tsp
Cumin powder ½ tsp
Chaat masala powder 1 tsp
Baking soda ¼ tsp
Salt 1 tsp
Black pepper, freshly ground 1 tsp
Oil for greasing

- Combine all the ingredients, except the oil, in a bowl and mix, till well blended.
- Cover and set aside in the refrigerator overnight.
- Grease a shallow baking tray with oil. Spread the kebab mix in the tray and flatten till about ¾" thick.
- Separate the mix with a spatula into 5" long, 1" wide strips. Leave ½" of space between the strips.
- Put the pan under a very hot grill for 8–10 minutes, till cooked through.
- Using a spatula, lift out the strips and arrange on a serving platter.
- Serve hot with steamed rice or naan (p. 33), sesame tomato chutney (p. 14) and a fresh garden salad.

VARIATION:
Ground beef may be used instead of mutton.

MELT-IN-THE-MOUTH KEBAB

GALOUTI KEBAB

Makes 2

Gilawatti (meaning that which melts in the mouth) or galouti kebab is one of the softest kebabs that literally melts in your mouth: a feast fit for kings. It is said that meat for the kebab is minced and ground a minimum of 13 times to get the desired texture.

There is no confirmed history on the origin of the galouti kebab, but the most accepted tale is that when the Nawab of Kakori, who craved meat, was old and toothless, the royal chefs were instructed to cook a meat dish the nawab could eat. After considerable thought, the meat was marinated with spices and minced 13 times to achieve the desired texture. I often joked with my great-grandmother, Maya, who lived till the age of 102, whenever it was made at home, saying, 'Here comes a kebab for a toothless queen.'

Today, galouti kebab is still a royal treat enjoyed by everyone. And here is the royal recipe for you.

Mutton, boneless 200 gm
Saffron strands 1/3 tsp
Warm milk 1 tsp
Onion, chopped fine 1 tsp
Ginger, chopped fine ½ tsp
Papaya, unripe, paste 1 tsp
Brown onion paste 1 tsp (p. 4)
Yogurt, hung, whisked 1½ tsp (p. 5)
Cream, fresh, thick 1 tsp
Gram flour, roasted 1 tsp
Coriander powder 1 tsp
Garam masala powder 1/3 tsp
Nutmeg powder 1/3 tsp
Salt 1½ tsp

Charcoal, red-hot 1 piece
Cloves 3
Ghee ½ tsp
Oil for shallow-frying
Chaat masala powder 1 tsp

- Pass the meat twice through the mincer to get a very fine mince.
- Soak the saffron strands in warm milk for 8–10 minutes.
- Put the mince in a bowl with the remaining ingredients for the kebabs, including the soaked saffron. Mix well to form a smooth paste.
- Cover and set aside in the refrigerator for 2 hours.
- Smoke the kebab mix as given on p. 44.
- Grease your hands lightly and divide the kebab mix into 4 equal portions. Shape them into balls and flatten them slightly at the centre.
- Heat the oil in a pan. Put the kebabs into the pan and shallow-fry on low heat till cooked through and brown on both sides.
- Drain on kitchen paper.
- Arrange the kebabs on a serving platter and sprinkle chaat masala powder on top.
- Serve hot with mint chutney (p. 12).

STUFFED MINCE PATTIES
SHIKAMPURI KEBAB

Makes 2

The perfect blend of spices with chana dal with a whiff of cardamom makes this a special dish. I learnt this from a Pakistani chef who had come to India for a culinary festival in Delhi. He educated me on how to perfect this dish and not to overstuff the mixture with the mince otherwise the kebab would crack. So here we go with one of the easy to cook but delicious recipes.

Mutton, leg, boneless 200 gm
Husked, split Bengal gram/chana dal 3 tbsp
Saffron strands 6
Green chilli, kept whole 1
Black cardamoms 2
Cinnamon 1" stick
Cloves 2
Bay leaves 3
Mint leaves, fresh, chopped 1 tsp
Lime juice 1 tsp
Ginger-garlic paste 1 tsp
Yellow chilli powder 1/3 tsp
Coriander powder 1/2 tsp
Chaat masala powder 1 tsp
Garam masala powder 1/2 tsp
Salt 1 tsp
Oil for shallow-frying
Chaat masala powder 1 tsp
Coriander leaves, fresh, chopped 1 tbsp

Filling
Onion, chopped fine 1/2 tsp
Ginger, chopped fine 1/2 tsp

Green chilli, chopped fine ½ tsp
Spinach, boiled, chopped fine ½ tsp
Salt 1 tsp
Black pepper powder 1 tsp

- Wash the meat, trim and drain thoroughly. Cut it into chunks.
- Wash the gram and drain it.
- Dissolve the saffron in 1 tbsp of water.
- Put the meat in a pan with the saffron, gram, green chilli, whole spices and bay leaves.
- Pour in enough water to cover the contents of the pan.
- Place the pan on low heat and cook till the meat is tender and the water has evaporated.
- Remove and discard the whole spices and bay leaves.
- Grind the cooked meat in a food processor to make a smooth paste.
- Transfer to a bowl and mix in the remaining ingredients for the kebabs.
- Combine the ingredients for the filling in a bowl and mix well.
- Wet your hands and shape the kebab mix into balls. Press a kebab ball in the centre, with your thumb to make an indentation. Put a portion of filling into it and cover the filling with the kebab mix. Shape the kebab into an oval patty.
- Make the remaining kebabs in the same way.
- Refrigerate to stiffen them.
- Heat the oil in a pan. Shallow-fry the kebabs on low heat, till golden brown on both sides.
- Drain on kitchen paper.
- Arrange the kebabs on a serving platter and sprinkle chaat masala powder and coriander leaves on top.
- Serve hot with mint chutney (p. 12) and a salad.

MINCED MUTTON KEBABS

SEEKH KEBAB

Makes 3–4

A North Indian speciality, this delicacy is also known as shish kebab in some parts of the world: a minced mutton preparation that melts in your mouth. This dish is close to my heart as it was the first kebab I learnt to cook from my grandfather at Moti Mahal in Daryaganj. Although easy to prepare, it took me some time to be able to shape the kebabs on to the skewers. I recommend eating it the way I have always enjoyed it—rolled in a naan or pita bread with onion rings and mint chutney. Yummy!

Mutton, minced 500 gm
Egg, whisked 1
Onion, chopped fine 1
Green chillies, chopped fine 2
Ginger, chopped fine 1 tsp
Red chilli powder ½ tbsp
Garam masala powder ½ tbsp
Salt 1 tsp
Oil, for basting 2 tbsp
Coriander leaves, fresh, chopped 2 tsp
Lime, cut into wedges 1

- Combine the ingredients for the kebabs in a bowl. Mix well.
- Wet your hands and a few long, thick metal skewers.
- Roll the kebab mix into 16 balls and thread them on to the skewers. Shape the balls into 2" long kebabs along the length of the skewers, 1" apart.
- Cook the kebabs in a hot tandoor; or grill over a charcoal fire; or under a medium-hot gas or electric grill as described on pp. xiv–xv for 7–8 minutes.

- Baste with oil, turn the skewers and grill again for another 8–10 minutes.
- Slip the kebabs off the skewers and arrange on a serving platter.
- Sprinkle coriander leaves on top and serve hot with lime wedges as a snack.

MINCED MUTTON KEBABS IN A CRISP COATING
SEEKH KEBAB GILAFI

Makes 6–8

Another version of seekh kebab, this time coated with onions, bell pepper and tomato. It's a delightful snack.

Mutton, minced 1 kg
Oil ¼ cup
Processed Cheddar cheese, grated 100 gm
Brown onion paste 200 gm (p. ***)
Green chillies, seeded, minced 6
Ginger paste 1½ tbsp
Garlic paste 1 tbsp
Garam masala powder 2 tsp
Red chilli powder 2 tsp
Salt 2 tsp
Butter, melted, for basting 3 tbsp
Onion, sliced in rings 1

Coating
Onion, medium-sized, chopped fine 1
Green bell pepper, medium-sized, chopped fine 2
Tomato, medium-sized, seeded, chopped fine 1

- Combine the ingredients for the kebabs in a bowl and mix thoroughly.
- Combine the coating ingredients in another bowl and mix well.
- Squeeze the kebab mix with your hands to remove any excess moisture.
- Wet your hands and a few long, thick metal skewers.
- Roll the kebab mix into 16 balls and thread them on to the

skewers. Shape the balls into 2" long kebabs along the length of the skewers, 1" apart.
- Press the coating mix into the kebabs.
- Cook the kebabs in a medium-hot tandoor; or grill under a very hot gas or electric grill as described on pp. xiv–xv for 10–12 minutes.
- Baste with melted butter, turn the skewers and grill again for another 2–3 minutes.
- Slip the kebabs off the skewers on to a serving platter.
- Serve hot with onion rings and mint chutney (p. 12).

PAPRIKA KEBABS

Makes 8–10

Paprika is a spice, made of Hungarian bell pepper. The seasoning is used in many cuisines to add colour and flavour to dishes, but it is usually associated with Hungary as well as some other parts of Europe such as Greece, Spain, Portugal, Serbia, Croatia, Bulgaria and Morocco. In Spanish, Paprika has been known as Pimenton. It was in Paris that I learnt this recipe from a Hungarian chef I met during the Paris Cook Book Fair, in the international show kitchen where I was demonstrating how to make chicken tikka masala. After my show he came onto the stage and gave me this special recipe which uses paprika. On returning home, I tried this Hungarian recipe and the result was phenomenal.

Mutton, ground 1 kg
Onions, medium-sized, grated 3
Garlic, crushed 6 cloves
Parsley, fresh, chopped ¼ cup
Mint leaves, dried 2 tsp
Cumin powder 1½ tsp
Red chilli powder 1½ tsp
Paprika 1 tsp
Salt 2½ tsp
Black pepper, freshly ground 1 tsp
Onion, sliced 1
Lime, cut into wedges 1

- Put the meat in a large bowl.
- Combine the remaining ingredients in another bowl and add them to the meat.
- Knead it into the meat, till well blended.
- Wet your hands and a few long, thick metal skewers.
- Roll the kebab mix into small balls and thread them on to the

skewers. Shape the balls into 2" long kebabs along the length of the skewers, 1" apart.

- Refrigerate the kebabs overnight, for the flavours to blend and to firm up the meat.
- Remove the meat from the refrigerator and bring to room temperature.
- Grill the kebabs under a medium-hot gas or electric grill as described on pp. xiv–xv, till brown.
- Turn the skewers and grill the other side, till brown.
- Serve hot with onion slices and lime wedges.
- Make wraps, pita sandwiches, or dip it in yogurt and eat as is.

NOTE:

Take care not to overcook the kebabs. Ground mutton can be lean, and the kebabs can get dry. (Add more yogurt as you eat them, if they do get too dry.)

ARABIAN HAMBURGER

KAFTA

Makes 2–4

This kebab is basically ground beef, chopped onions, parsley and spices, wrapped around a skewer and cooked over a grill. I tried this once at a restaurant in Lebanon which boasted of this being their signature dish. It really was!

Mutton, ground 500 gm
Olive oil 1 tbsp
Onions, chopped fine ½ cup
Garlic, large, minced 3 cloves
Parsley, fresh, chopped fine ½ cup
Mint leaves, dried 1 tsp
Oregano, dried ½ tsp
Cumin powder 1 tsp
Coriander powder ½ tsp
Salt 1½ tsp
Black pepper, freshly ground ½ tsp
Oil, for basting 2 tbsp
Onion, sliced 1

- Combine the ingredients for the kebabs in a bowl. Mix thoroughly, till they blend well.
- Refrigerate for about 1 hour to firm up the mix.
- Wet your hands and a few long, thick metal skewers.
- Roll the kebab mix into 24 small balls and thread them on to the skewers. Shape the balls into 2" long kebabs along the length of the skewers, 1" apart.
- Grill under a medium-hot gas or electric grill as described on pp. xiv–xv for 5–7 minutes.
- Baste with oil, turn the skewers and grill again for another 5 minutes.
- Slip the kafta off the skewers on to a serving dish.
- Serve hot with onion slices, pita bread (p. 24) and a garlic dip.

IRANIAN MINCED MUTTON
CHELOW KEBAB

Makes 3–4

While in Turkey I met an Iranian family at a nightclub, enjoying traditional food watching a Turkish cultural programme. Interestingly, we were served chelow kebab, which is the national dish of Iran, at the buffet. *Chelow* in Farsi means rice and sounds similar to *chawal* in Hindi.

I prefer to grill these kebabs over a charcoal grill rather than a gas one, since the flavour is considerably enhanced. The meat juices drip on to the charcoal and the vapours rising from the coal create a smoked flavour in the kebabs. In the absence of a charcoal grill, use your oven grill.

Mutton, ground 500 gm
Onion, large, chopped fine 1
Lime juice 1 tsp
Cumin powder 1 tsp
Black pepper, freshly ground ½ tsp
Salt 2 tsp
Oil, for basting 2 tbsp

- Combine the ingredients for the kebabs in a bowl. Mix well, using two wooden spoons or your hands.
- Wet your hands and a few long, thick metal skewers.
- Roll the kebab mix into 4 balls and thread them on to the skewers. Shape the balls into 2" long kebabs along the length of the skewers, 1" apart.
- Grill over a charcoal fire; or under a very hot gas or electric grill as described on pp. xiv–xv for about 5 minutes.
- Baste with oil, turn the skewers and grill again for another 5 minutes.

- Serve the kebabs over a bed of white steamed rice, Persian rice or with pita bread (p. 24) and a salad on the side.

VARIATION:
Ground beef may be used instead of mutton.

IRANIAN MINCED MUTTON KEBABS

KEBAB-E-KUBIDEH

Makes 4

Farsi was once a scholar's language. It later became quite popular and I remember my grandfather talking to his friends in Farsi. Since he was a chef, he taught me several Iranian recipes and this was one of his favourites. It is made from ground mutton, beef or chicken, often mixed with parsley and chopped onions.

Mutton, ground 750 gm
Onions, medium, grated 2½
Egg, whisked 1
Cardamom powder 1 tsp
Salt 1½ tsp
Black pepper, freshly ground 1 tsp
Tomatoes, medium-sized, kept whole 5
Oil, for basting 2 tbsp

- Mix the meat, onions, egg, cardamom powder, salt and pepper well in a bowl and leave in the refrigerator overnight or for several hours.
- Remove the meat from the refrigerator and bring to room temperature.
- Wet your hands and a few long, thick metal skewers.
- Roll the kebab mix into balls and thread them on to the skewers. Shape the balls into 2" long kebabs along the length of the skewers, 1" apart.
- Thread the whole tomatoes on to another skewer.
- Grill under a very hot gas or electric grill (pp. xiv–xv) for about 5 minutes.
- Baste with oil, turn the skewers and grill again for another 5 minutes.
- Collect any juices that may have dripped into the grill pan.
- (If skewers are not available, kebab-e-kubideh can be shaped

into long, thin sausages on aluminium foil and grilled along with the tomatoes.)
- Sprinkle the reserved cooking juices over the kebabs.
- Serve over hot chelow (Persian rice) or on pita bread (p. 24) with mint chutney (p. 12) and a salad of your choice.
- If serving with rice, sprinkle some sumac or lime juice on top.

VARIATION:
Ground beef may be used instead of mutton.

MINCED MUTTON KEBABS IN PITA WRAPS

BEYTI KEBAB

Makes 4–6

This famous Turkish kebab was created in the renowned Beyti Kebab House in Istanbul. I visited the place, which was founded by Mr Beyti Güler, probably one of the first chefs in Turkey whose name has been given to a signature dish.

Closely resembling our seekh kebab, it is made with marinated minced mutton grilled on a skewer and is often wrapped in lavash and topped with tomato sauce and yogurt.

Mutton, ground 700 gm
Lime juice 1 tsp
Cumin powder 2 tsp
Coriander powder 2 tsp
Red chilli flakes 1 tsp
Salt 3 tsp
Black pepper, freshly ground 2 tsp
Olive oil, for basting 3 tbsp

Tomato sauce
Olive oil 3 tbsp
Onion, chopped fine 1
Tomato, sliced fine 1
Tomato sauce, commercial 200 ml
Cumin powder ½ tsp
Salt 1 tsp
Black pepper, freshly ground ¼ tsp

To wrap
Pita bread, very thin (p. 24)

Dip
Yogurt, hung, whisked 1 cup (p. 5)

Olive oil 2 tbsp
Parsley, fresh, chopped 2 tbsp

- Combine the ingredients for the kebabs in a bowl.
- Mix well and set aside in the refrigerator for 2-3 hours.

Tomato sauce
- Heat the oil in a pan. Add the onion and sauté over medium heat for about 3 minutes.
- Add the remaining sauce ingredients.
- Stir for about 5–6 minutes, till the oil leaves the sides of the pan.
- Remove from heat and keep warm.

For the kebabs
- Remove the kebab mix from the refrigerator and bring to room temperature.
- Form the mix into 1" thick, 6" wide patties.
- Brush the meat patties with olive oil.
- Grill the patties under a medium hot grill for about 15–20 minutes, turning and basting with oil frequently.
- The meat is ready when it is springy to the touch.
- Wrap the meat patties twice in thin pita bread.
- Cut the wraps into bite-sized pieces and arrange them in a circle on a plate.
- Lightly drizzle the tomato sauce over the wrapped meat inside the pita bread.
- Whisk the yogurt and olive oil together, till well blended and pour it into a small bowl.
- Sprinkle parsley on top and place the bowl in the centre of the plate of wrapped meat, to serve as a dip.

VARIATION:
A mix of ground mutton and veal may be used instead of only mutton.

MINCED MUTTON WITH
AUBERGINE PURÉE

ALI NAZIK KEBABI

Makes 4

This kebab is sautéed ground meat served on a bed of puréed
aubergine. As a true Punjabi, my mouth waters at the thought of
baingan bharta (Indian puréed aubergines) with crisp tandoori
roti, white butter and a mango pickle. Perhaps that is why I like
this particular Turkish kebab. I relish it with Norwegian flatbread
(p. 27) made with buttermilk which imparts a soft buttery taste;
again a Punjabi trait.

Aubergine purée
Aubergines, medium-sized, long, thin 4
Oil 1 tbsp
Yogurt, hung, whisked 2½ cups (p. ***)
Garlic, minced 3 cloves
Tomatoes, peeled, chopped fine 2
Green cardamom powder ½ tsp
Salt 1 tsp

Kebabs
Butter 1 tbsp
Mutton, ground 500 gm
Red chilli powder ½ tsp
Coriander powder 1 tsp
Black pepper, freshly ground 1 tsp
Salt 2 tsp
Green bell pepper, large, chopped 1
Red bell pepper, large, chopped 1

Aubergine purée
- Roast the aubergines over a flame to char the skin, turning
  frequently.

- Cool and peel off the skin. Mince the flesh.
- Heat the oil in a pan and sauté the aubergine flesh for 3 minutes on medium heat, stirring continuously.
- Add the remaining ingredients for the purée and mix thoroughly.
- Remove from heat and keep warm.

For the kebabs
- Melt the butter in a pan on low to medium heat. Add the meat and brown it well, till cooked through.
- Add the spice powders and salt and mix well.
- Spread the aubergine purée evenly in a shallow serving dish. Arrange the ground meat in the centre.
- Top with the chopped bell pepper and serve warm with Irani raita (p. 19), onion rings and Norwegian flatbread (p. 27).

VARIATION:
Ground beef may be used instead of mutton.

RAJASTHANI BOTI KEBAB

Makes 2

Mutton, boneless 250 gm

First Marinade
Papaya, unripe, paste 1 tbsp
Ginger-garlic paste 1 tbsp
White vinegar 1 tsp
Red chilli powder ½ tsp
Salt ½ tsp

Second marinade
Yogurt, hung, whisked 2 tbsp (p. 5)
Oil 2 tsp
Ginger-garlic paste 1 tsp
Fenugreek leaves, dried, powdered ⅓ tsp
Garam masala powder ⅓ tsp
Cinnamon powder ⅓ tsp
Green cardamom powder ⅓ tsp
Salt ½ tsp

For the kebabs
Ghee, melted, for basting 2 tbsp
Coriander leaves, fresh, chopped 1 tbsp

- Wash the meat, pat dry with paper towels and trim. Cut it into 2" cubes.
-

First marination
- Combine the ingredients for the first marinade in a bowl and whisk, till well blended.
- Add the meat and mix well, to ensure that it is completely coated with the marinade.

- Cover and set aside to marinate in the refrigerator for about 1 hour.

Second marination
- Whisk the yogurt in a bowl with the remaining ingredients for the second marinade.
- Squeeze the marinated meat with your hands to remove excess moisture.
- Add it to the bowl and mix well, to ensure that it is completely coated with the second marinade.
- Cover and set aside to marinate in the refrigerator for 4–5 hours

For the kebabs
- Remove the meat from the refrigerator and bring to room temperature.
- Thread the meat on to long, thin metal skewers, 1" apart.
- Grill the kebabs under a very hot gas or electric grill as described on pp. xiv–xv for 8–10 minutes.
- Baste with melted ghee, turn the skewers and grill again for another 7–8 minutes.
- Slip the kebabs off the skewers on to a serving platter.
- Sprinkle coriander leaves on top and serve hot with mint chutney (p. 12) .

FENUGREEK MUTTON KEBABS

Makes 6–8

Fenugreek (methi) has three culinary uses: as a herb (dried or fresh leaves), as a spice (seeds), and as a vegetable (fresh leaves, sprouts and micro-greens).

The distinctive cuboid-shaped, amber-coloured fenugreek seeds are frequently encountered in the cuisines of the Indian subcontinent. It can be used whole or powdered and should be roasted to enhance its flavour and reduce bitterness. This unique blend of spices with fenugreek dominating the aroma enhances the flavour of these kebabs.

Mutton, leg or shoulder, boneless 1 kg

First marinade
Ginger-garlic paste 6 tbsp
White vinegar 3 tbsp
Red chilli powder 2 tbsp
Salt 4 tsp
Black pepper powder 1 tsp

Second marinade
Cream, fresh, whisked 3 tbsp
Processed Cheddar cheese 3 tbsp
Fenugreek leaves, dried, powdered (kasuri methi) ½ tsp
Fenugreek seeds, powdered 2 tsp
Saffron strands 2–3
Garam masala powder 1 tsp
Coriander powder 1 tsp
Cumin powder 1 tsp

For the kebabs
Oil, for basting 3 tbsp
Coriander leaves, fresh, chopped 2 tbsp
Lime, cut into wedges 2

- Wash the meat, trim and drain thoroughly. Cut it into 1" cubes.

First marination
- Combine the ingredients for the first marinade in a bowl and whisk, till well blended.
- Add the meat and mix well to ensure that it is completely coated with the marinade.
- Cover and set aside to marinate in the refrigerator for about 2 hours.

Second marination
- Combine the ingredients for the second marinade in another bowl and whisk, till well blended.
- Add the marinated meat to the bowl and mix well, to ensure that it is completely coated with the second marinade.
- Cover and set aside to marinate in the refrigerator for about 1 hour.

For the kebabs
- Remove the meat from the refrigerator and bring to room temperature.
- Thread the meat on to long, thin metal skewers, 1" apart.
- Grill the kebabs over a charcoal fire, or under a medium-hot gas or electric grill as described on pp. xiv–xv for about 10 minutes.
- Baste with oil, turn the skewers and grill again for another 5 minutes.
- Slip the kebabs off the skewers on to a serving platter.
- Sprinkle coriander leaves on top and serve hot with lime wedges on the side.

NORTHWEST FRONTIER
MUTTON KEBABS

BURRAH KEBAB

Makes 6–8

A popular dish on the Moti Mahal menu. The trick is to marinate the mutton overnight with unripe papaya paste in the first marinade, to get a tender, mouth-watering kebab.

Mutton, boneless 1 kg
Oil for basting
Chaat masala powder 1½ tsp
Coriander leaves, fresh, chopped 1 tbsp

First marinade
Ginger-garlic paste 1 tbsp
Papaya, unripe, paste 1 tbsp
Kachri powder ½ tbsp (see note)

Second marinade
Yogurt, hung, whisked ½ cup (p. 5)
Mustard oil 3 tbsp
Meat masala (commercial) 2 tbsp
Cumin powder ½ tbsp
Garam masala powder ½ tbsp
Red Kashmiri chilli powder 2 tsp
Salt 1 tbsp
Black salt ¼ tbsp

• Wash the meat, pat dry with paper towels and trim. Cut it into 2" cubes.

First marination
• Combine the ingredients for the first marinade in a bowl and whisk, till well blended.

- Add the meat and mix well, to ensure that it is completely coated with the marinade.
- Cover and set aside to marinate in the refrigerator for 3–4 hours.

Second marination
- Combine the ingredients for the second marinade in another bowl and whisk, till well blended.
- Add the marinated meat to the bowl and mix well, to ensure that it is completely coated with the second marinade.
- Cover and set aside to marinate in the refrigerator for about 12 hours.

For the kebabs
- Remove the meat from the refrigerator and bring to room temperature.
- Thread the meat on to long, thin metal skewers, 1" apart.
- Grill the kebabs under a very hot gas or electric grill as described on pp. xiv–xv for about 10 minutes.
- Baste with oil, turn the skewers and grill again for another 7–8 minutes.
- Slip the kebabs off the skewers on to a serving platter.
- Sprinkle chaat masala powder and coriander leaves on top and serve hot with mint chutney (p. 12).

NOTE:
Kachri is a wild variety of cucumber that grows in desert areas and resembles small, yellow-brown melons. If it is not available, increase the unripe papaya paste to 1½ tbsp.

MUTTON KEBABS FROM PESHAWAR
PESHAWARI BOTI KEBAB

Makes 6–8

This is my grandparents' treasured recipe from Peshawar,
Pakistan, where they lived before Independence. My grandfather
cooked it to perfection and it is dedicated to him in this book.

Mutton, boneless 250 gm
Oil, for frying 1½ cups
Coriander leaves, fresh, chopped 1 tsp

First Marinade
Papaya, unripe, paste 1 tbsp
Ginger-garlic paste 1 tbsp
Red chilli powder ½ tsp
Salt 2 tsp

Second marinade
Yogurt, hung, whisked 4 tsp (p. 5)
Ginger-garlic paste ½ tsp
Gram flour, roasted 1 tsp
Fenugreek leaves, dried, powdered ⅓ tsp
Cumin powder ½ tsp
Red chilli powder ⅓ tsp
Garam masala powder ⅓ tsp
Black pepper, crushed 1 tsp
Salt 2 tsp

- Wash the meat, pat dry with paper towels and trim. Cut it into
  2" cubes.

First marination
- Combine the ingredients for the first marinade in a bowl and
  whisk, till well blended.

- Add the meat and mix well, to ensure that it is completely coated with the marinade.
- Cover and set aside to marinate in the refrigerator for 1½ hours.

Second marination
- Whisk the yogurt in a bowl with the remaining ingredients for the second marinade.
- Squeeze the marinated meat with your hands to remove excess moisture.
- Add it to the bowl and mix well, to ensure that the pieces are completely coated with the second marinade.
- Cover and set aside to marinate in the refrigerator for 4–5 hours

For the kebabs
- Remove the meat from the refrigerator and bring to room temperature.
- Heat the oil in a pan. Add the meat and stir-fry on medium heat for a few seconds.
- Cover the pan and cook on very low heat for about 15 minutes.
- Open the pan and raise heat to medium. Toss the meat pieces periodically, till golden-brown.
- Drain on kitchen paper.
- Sprinkle coriander leaves on top and serve hot with mint chutney (p. 12) and a salad.

MUTTON TIKKA MASALA

Makes 2–3

The words of Mr Marsden, then Director of the British Council in Delhi, still echo in my ears: 'The bird has truly migrated' after his first bite of chicken tikka masala. The butter chicken which was invented by my grandfather, Kundan Lal Gujral, was adapted by the British as chicken tikka masala, now referred to as a national dish in Britain.

This is my twist with mutton. The succulent mutton grilled to perfection and cooked to perfection in the tikka masala

Mutton, boneless 300 gm
Oil, for basting 2 tbsp
Coriander leaves, fresh, chopped 2 tbsp

First marinade
Papaya, unripe, paste 2 tbsp
Ginger–garlic paste 2 tsp
Red chilli paste 2 tbsp
White vinegar 2 tsp
Refined oil 1 tbsp
Salt 1 tsp

Second marinade
Yogurt, hung, whisked ²/₃ cup (p. 5)
Lime juice 2 tbsp
Red chilli paste 2 tsp
Garam masala powder 2 tbsp
Salt 1 tsp
White pepper powder 1 tbsp

Tikka masala
Oil 2 tsp
Onion, medium-sized, chopped 2
Ginger-garlic paste 1 tbsp
Green cardamoms 3
Black cardamoms 2
Cloves 3
Mace flakes 2
Bay leaf 1
Red degi chilli powder 2 tsp
Cumin powder 1 tsp
Chaat masala powder 1 tsp
Garam masala powder 1½ tsp
Salt 1 tsp
Tomato, medium-sized, puréed 1
Green chilli–coriander paste 2 tbsp (see note)
Green bell peppers, chopped 2
Lime juice 1 tsp
Butter 40 gm
Cream, fresh, whisked ½ cup

- Wash the meat, trim and drain well. Cut it into 8 slices. Put the slices between wet cling-film sheets and flatten them with a mallet or rolling pin into 4" long, 2"–3" wide pasanda.

First marination
- Combine the ingredients for the first marinade in a bowl and whisk, till well blended.
- Add the meat and mix well, to ensure that it is completely coated with the marinade.
- Cover and set aside to marinate in the refrigerator for about 2 hours.

Second marination
- Whisk the yogurt in a bowl with the remaining ingredients for the second marinade.

- Squeeze the marinated mutton slices with your hands to remove excess moisture.
- Add them to the bowl and mix well, to ensure that the slices are completely coated with the second marinade.
- Cover and set aside to marinate in the refrigerator for another 3 hours.

For the kebabs
- Remove the meat from the refrigerator and bring to room temperature.
- Thread the meat slices on to long, thin metal skewers, 1" apart.
- Coat the slices with any remaining marinade.
- Cook the kebabs in a medium-hot tandoor; or grill under a hot gas or electric grill as described on pp. xiv–xv for about 10 minutes.
- Baste with oil, turn the skewers and grill again for another 5 minutes.
- Set aside.

The masala
- While the kebabs are being cooked, make the masala.
- Heat the oil in a wok. Add the onion and sauté on medium heat, till golden brown.
- Mix in the ginger–garlic paste, whole spices and bay leaf and sauté for 2–3 minutes.
- Stir in the spice powders and salt.
- Add the cooked meat and sauté for about 5 minutes.
- Mix in the tomato purée, green chilli–coriander paste, bell peppers and lime juice and stir for 3–4 minutes.
- Blend in the butter and sauté for 2 minutes.
- Mix in the cream and remove the pan from the heat.

To serve
- Spoon the kebabs on to a serving platter.
- Sprinkle coriander leaves on top and serve hot.

NOTE:

To make the **green chilli–coriander paste**, grind 1 green chilli with 2 tbsp chopped coriander leaves and ½ tbsp of water in a food processor. This should give you 2 tbsp of the paste.

SUYA OR *TSIRE* KEBAB

Makes 3–4

This is a West African kebab or grilled meat preparation, also known as *chichinga* in Ghana. It is a popular barbeque street food in several West African countries. I recommend using roasted peanuts in the marinade as it imparts a special flavour to the dish. Suya can be made with beef, chicken, goat meat or any other meat of your choice.

Mutton, boneless 500 gm

Marinade
Peanuts, roasted 3 tbsp
Ginger, fresh, grated or dried, powder 1 tsp
Red chilli powder 1 tsp
Paprika powder 1 tsp
Garlic powder 1 tsp
Coriander powder ½ tsp
Bouillon soup cube, crumbled 1
Salt 2 tsp

- Wash the meat, pat dry with paper towels and trim. Cut it into bite-sized pieces.

Marination
- Grind the roasted peanuts in a food processor to make a fine powder
- Add the remaining ingredients for the marinade, except the salt and grind again, to ensure that the marinade is well blended. Taste and add salt.
- Transfer to a bowl.
- Add the meat and mix well, to ensure that it is completely coated with the marinade.

- Cover and set aside in the refrigerator to marinate overnight.

For the kebabs
- Remove the meat from the refrigerator and bring to room temperature.
- Thread the meat on to long, thin metal skewers, 1" apart.
- Grill the kebabs under a hot gas or electric grill as described on pp. xiv–xv for 12–15 minutes.
- Baste with the leftover marinade, turn the skewers and grill again, till the meat is tender.
- Slip the kebabs off the skewers on to a serving platter.
- Serve hot with sliced onions and a garlic dip.

MUTTON KEBABS WITH YOGURT
YOGURTLU KEBAB

Makes 4

This is a famous Turkish kebab served in restaurants and also prepared at home. On my recent trip to Turkey, I was invited by a friend to his home, where the family served this delicacy and claimed that it was their ancestral recipe. I dedicate this dish to my friend in Turkey.

Mutton, boneless 500 gm
Parsley, fresh, chopped 1 tbsp

Marinade
Onion juice ½ cup (see note)
Olive oil ¼ cup
Lime juice 1 tbsp
Red chilli powder 1 tsp
Salt 2 tsp
Black pepper powder 1 tsp

Tomato sauce
Tomatoes, ripe 3
Butter 1 tbsp
Salt 1 tsp
White vinegar ½ tsp

Green chillies
Green chillies 4
Salt ¼ tsp
Red chilli powder ¼ tsp
Malt vinegar 2 tbsp
Oil 1 tsp

To assemble the dish
Bread slices 4
Butter 2 tbsp
Yogurt, hung, whisked 2 cups (p. 5)

- Wash the meat, pat dry with paper towels and trim. Cut it into 1" cubes.

Marination

- Combine the ingredients for the marinade in a bowl and whisk, till well blended.
- Add the meat and mix well, to ensure that it is completely coated with the marinade.
- Cover and set aside to marinate in the refrigerator for 6–8 hours.

Tomato sauce

- Blanch the tomatoes and peel them. Chop fine and place them in a pan with the butter, salt and vinegar.
- Cook the tomatoes, stirring periodically, till they are soft and pulpy. Remove from heat and keep warm.

Green chillies

- Slit the green chillies and put them into a bowl. Add the salt, chilli powder and vinegar and rub them into the chillies.
- Put the oil in a small pan over low heat. Add the green chillies and toss, till they discolour slightly.
- Remove from heat and set aside to cool.

For the kebabs

- Remove the meat from the refrigerator and bring to room temperature.
- Thread the meat on to long, thin metal skewers, 1" apart.
- Grill over a charcoal fire; or under a very hot gas or electric grill as described on pp. xiv–xv for 10–15 minutes.
- Baste with the leftover marinade, turn the skewers and grill again for another 10 minutes.

- Toast the bread slices and cut them into small squares. Distribute them between the serving plates.
- Melt the butter and pour it over the bread. Spoon the hot tomato sauce on top, followed by the whisked yogurt.
- Slip the kebabs off the skewers and place them on the plates alongside the bread.
- Sprinkle the parsley and the prepared green chillies on top and serve hot.

NOTE:

To make onion juice, chop 2–3 onions roughly and extract the juice using a juicer. Strain and use. This should give you ½ cup of onion juice.

TANGY MEAT KEBABS

CHISLIC

Makes 2–3

I was invited by a Facebook community called Toxos, which celebrates good food and cooking, to Frankfurt in 2011. It was formed by my friend, Stefan Bauman, a culinary enthusiast. There I met a wonderful Russian chef from whom I learned this recipe. He informed me that it was a German–Russian fusion kebab introduced by German immigrants to Russia.

Mutton 1 kg
Red chilli flakes ½ tsp
Garlic, chopped 50 gm
Salt, a small bowl
Hot chilli sauce (p. 16)

Marinade
A zesty Italian dressing (commercial) 1¼ cups
French dressing (commercial) 1¼ cups
Oregano, dried ½ tsp

- Wash the meat and pat dry with paper towels. Trim and remove all fat. Cut the meat into bite-sized pieces.

Marination
- Combine the ingredients for the marinade in a bowl and whisk, till they blend well.
- Add the meat and mix well, to ensure that it is completely coated with the marinade.
- Cover and set aside to marinate in the refrigerator overnight.

For the chislic
- Remove the meat from the refrigerator and bring to room temperature.

- Soak wooden skewers in water for 20 minutes. Drain and set aside.
- Drain the meat from the marinade.
- Thread it evenly on to the soaked and drained wooden skewers, 1" apart.
- Grill the kebabs under a very hot gas or electric grill as described on pp. xiv–xv, till cooked to the desired degree— rare, medium-rare or well done. (Chislic is usually served medium-rare.)
- Arrange the skewers on a serving platter and sprinkle chilli flakes on top.
- Serve with the garlic, salt and hot chilli sauce passed around separately.

NOTE:

Alternatively chislic can be deep-fried, without threading them on to skewers, and served wrapped in pita bread (p. 24) with onion slices on the side.

VARIATION:

Beef may be used instead of mutton.

STEAMED KEBABS

BUGU KEBABI

Makes 4–6

Truly a Turkish delight! This one is for weight-watchers as the kebab is steamed in a style similar to the Indian dumpukht. An aromatic kebab, I may call it the neighbours' envy because whenever I cook it, the aromas make my neighbours' mouths water.

Mutton, boneless 1 kg
Butter 120 gm
Onions, very small or shallots, kept whole 500 gm
Tomatoes, sliced 4
Bay leaf 1
Thyme, dried 1 tsp
Salt 1½ tsp
Black peppercorns, whole 5
White pepper, freshly ground 1 tsp
Parsley, fresh, chopped 2 tbsp

Sealing dough
Refined flour/maida 150 gm

- Wash the meat, trim and drain thoroughly. Cut it into 1" cubes.
- Put the meat into a pan that has a tight-fitting lid, with the remaining kebab ingredients and 1 cup of water.
- Sift the flour into a bowl. Gradually add water and mix to make a soft dough.
- Roll the dough into a long sausage and stick it around the rim of the pan. Put the lid firmly over the dough and press it in to seal the pan.

- Put the pan on medium heat and cook for about 1½ hours, till the meat is tender.
- Open the pan and transfer to a serving dish.
- Sprinkle parsley on top and serve hot with steamed rice or garlic flatbread (p. 31) and Irani raita (p. 19).

GARDENER'S KEBABS
BAHCIVAN KEBABI

Makes 4–6

Again a Turkish wonder. Especially for those, like me, who love their meat with fresh garden veggies. A beautifully balanced colourful kebab, enjoy it with Turkish lavash (p. 29).

Mutton, shoulder or leg, boneless 1 kg
Olive oil, extra virgin; or refined oil ½ cup
Onions, medium-sized, chopped fine 2½
Tomato paste, commercial 2½ cups
Salt 2 tsp
Black pepper, freshly ground 1 tsp
Carrots, medium-sized, cut into ½" cubes 2
Potatoes, medium-sized, cut into ½" cubes 3
Green peas, shelled ½ cup
Coriander leaves, fresh, chopped 2 tbsp
Parsley, fresh, chopped 1 tbsp

- Wash the meat, trim and drain thoroughly. Cut it into ¾" cubes.
- Heat the oil in a pan. Add the meat with the onions.
- Cover the pan and cook on low heat for about 1 hour, stirring occasionally.
- Strain the meat and transfer it to a fresh pan.
- Add the tomato paste and 1 cup of hot water. Sprinkle with salt and pepper.
- Cover the pan and simmer for 15–20 minutes on low to medium heat.
- Add the carrots, potatoes, green peas and coriander leaves and mix gently.
- Cover and cook for 30 minutes, till the meat and vegetables are tender.
- Spoon the meat and vegetables into a serving dish and sprinkle parsley on top.
- Serve hot with sesame tomato chutney (p. 14).

CLAY POT KEBAB
TESTI KEBAB

Makes 2–3

An authentic Turkish recipe for testi kebabs, which are an Anatolian speciality. They are prepared in a handmade clay pot which preserves the aroma, freshness and flavours of the vegetables and meat, since the ingredients are cooked in their own steam. Special clay pots are made by experienced artisans to cook testi kebabs. The pots are fired at 800°C for nearly 12 hours and have a clear breaking line marked on them. The pot is broken open with just a knock on the line, once the dish is ready.

Interestingly, one can relate this to the dumpukht style of cooking. I always advocate that we adapt our cooking methods to the availability of the local produce of a region.

Mutton, without fat 500 gm
Tomatoes, medium-sized 4
Green bell peppers, medium-sized 3
Green chillies, seeded, slit 2
Ginger, julienned 1 tsp
Garlic, chopped 10 small cloves
Salt 2 tsp
Whole black pepper 1½ tbsp
Local flavourings (oregano, rosemary, mint) to taste
Butter 50 gm

Sealing dough
Refined flour/maida 4 cups
Salt a pinch
Oil 1 tbsp

• Wash the meat, pat dry with paper towels and trim. Cut it into 1" cubes.

- Cut the tomatoes and bell peppers into 1" pieces.
- Combine the meat, vegetables, green chillies, ginger, garlic, salt and pepper in a bowl. Add the local flavourings and mix well.
- Wash a testi clay pot thoroughly and fill it with the kebab mix. Add butter.
- To make the sealing dough, combine the flour with salt and 1 cup of water in a bowl and mix well. Add the oil and knead to make a pliable dough.
- Cover the pot with the sealing dough and make a small hole at the centre to allow for air circulation.

For the kebabs
- Preheat the grill to very hot and place the pot inside.
- Grill for about 30 minutes.
- Remove the pot from the grill and leave it to stand for 5–10 minutes.
- Break open the pot by knocking it with the back of a kitchen knife along the specified breaking line and serve immediately from the pot with chilli garlic chutney (p. 11).

VARIATION:
Beef may be used instead of mutton.

SLICED MUTTON KEBAB

LUCKNOWI PASANDA KEBAB

Makes 6–8

A popular North Indian and Pakistani dish, this was a favourite with the Mughal emperors. 'Pasanda' is a variation of the Urdu word 'pasandé' or 'the favourite one', which refers to the traditional prime cut of meat—leg of mutton—sliced, flattened, marinated and fried with spicy, aromatic seasonings. Today, pasanda is also made with chicken and paneer.

My father was particularly fond of this dish and I learned it from him. He was a great visionary who inherited the Moti Mahal brand from my grandfather and founded the Moti Mahal Delux restaurant chain.

Mutton, boneless 1 kg
Oil, for basting 3 tbsp
Coriander leaves, fresh, chopped 1 tbsp

First marinade
Papaya, unripe, paste 3 tbsp
Ginger-garlic paste 2 tbsp
Garam masala powder 1 tsp
White pepper powder 1 tsp
Salt 4 tsp

Second marinade
Egg white, whisked 1
Cream, fresh, whisked 250 ml
Green cardamom powder ½ tsp
Nutmeg powder 1 tsp
Coriander powder 1 tsp
Cashew nut paste ½ cup (see note)
Green chillies, seeded, chopped 3–4

- Wash the meat, pat dry with paper towels and trim. Cut it into 2" slices, ½" thick.
- Put the slices between wet cling-film sheets and flatten them with a mallet or rolling pin into 4" long, 2"–3" wide pasanda.

First marination
- Combine the ingredients for the first marinade in a bowl and whisk, till they blend well.
- Add the meat and mix well, to ensure that it is completely coated with the marinade.
- Cover and set aside to marinate in the refrigerator for about 2 hours.

Second marination
- Whisk the egg white, cream and spice powders, till well blended. Add the cashew nut paste and green chillies and stir till blended.
- Add the marinated meat and mix well, to ensure that it is completely coated with the second marinade.
- Cover and set aside to marinate in the refrigerator for another 2 hours.

For the kebabs
- Remove the meat from the refrigerator and bring to room temperature.
- Thread the meat on to long, thin metal skewers, 1" apart.
- Cook the kebabs in a hot tandoor or grill over a charcoal fire or under a very hot gas or electric grill as described on pp. xiv–xv for about 10 minutes.
- Baste with oil, turn the skewers and grill again for another 5 minutes.
- Slip the kebabs off the skewers on to a serving platter, sprinkle coriander leaves on top and serve hot.

> **NOTE:**
> To make the cashew nut paste, grind 3 tbsp of cashew nuts with ¼ cup of milk to make a smooth paste.

SLICED MUTTON KEBABS
KEBAB-E-BARG

Makes 6–8

Again, an Iranian beauty. Barbecued mutton, chicken or beef kebabs, the main ingredients for kebab barg—a short form of its name—are fillets of beef tenderloin, mutton shank or chicken breast, onions and olive oil. The trick is to marinate the meat long enough for it to become tender and juicy.

I recommend this dish for a special dinner party when one wants to fish for compliments.

Mutton, boneless 1 kg
Olive oil, for basting 3 tbsp

Marinade
Olive oil ½ cup
Onions, large, chopped fine 3
Saffron strands ½ tsp
Ginger paste 1 tsp
Garlic paste 2 tbsp
Cumin powder 1 tsp
Salt 4 tsp
Black pepper, freshly ground 2 tbsp

• Wash the meat, pat dry with paper towels and trim. Cut it into ½" wide and 2"–2½" long slices.

Marination
• Combine the ingredients for the marinade in a bowl and whisk, till well blended.
• Add the meat and mix well, to ensure that it is completely coated with the marinade.
• Cover and set aside to marinate in the refrigerator for at least 12 hours.

For the kebabs

- Remove the meat from the refrigerator and bring to room temperature.
- Thread the meat on to long, thin metal skewers, keeping the pieces 1" apart.
- Grill under a very hot gas or electric grill as described on pp. xiv–xv for 5–6 minutes.
- Baste with oil, turn the skewers and grill again for another 7–8 minutes.
- Slip the kebabs off the skewers and serve hot with Irani raita (p. 19) and pita bread (p. 24). I tried it with rosemary flatbread (p. 32). The combination, with a hint of rosemary aroma, was outstanding.

SOUTHEAST ASIAN BARBECUE
SATAY

Makes 3–4

Originally, satay was a South East Asian dish of diced or sliced meat, skewered and grilled over a charcoal fire and served with various spicy seasonings. I normally recommend it as a starter. Meat, chicken, soy nuggets or beef can be used according to your choice.

Mutton, boneless 500 gm
Red chilli powder ½ tsp
Salt 1 tsp
Black pepper, freshly ground 1 tsp

First marinade
Ginger, grated 2 tsp
Garlic, crushed 3 cloves
Lemongrass, chopped ½ stalk
Coconut milk 2 tsp
Olive oil 1 tsp

Second marinade
Red chillies, dried, seeded, pounded 3
Coriander seeds, ground 1 tsp
Olive oil 1 tbsp
Coconut milk 3 tbsp
Tamarind paste or lime juice 1 tbsp
Soy sauce 1 tsp
Sugar 1 tbsp

For the satay
Coconut milk, for basting 2 tbsp
Hot satay peanut sauce (p. 16)

- Wash the meat, trim and drain thoroughly. Slice the meat against the grain into 6" long, 1" wide strips.

First marination
- Grind the ginger, garlic and lemongrass to make a smooth paste.
- Transfer to a bowl and mix in the coconut milk and oil.
- Add the meat and mix well, to ensure that it is completely coated with the marinade.
- Cover and set aside to marinate in the refrigerator for 4–5 hours.

Second marination
- Combine the ingredients for the second marinade in a food processor and grind to make a fine paste.
- Soak wooden skewers in water for 20 minutes and drain them.
- Remove the meat from the refrigerator and thread it on to the soaked and drained skewers.
- Spread the second marinade evenly over the skewered meat.
- Place the skewers on a plate, cover and refrigerate for 2 hours, spreading more paste if necessary.

For the kebabs
- Remove the skewers from the refrigerator and bring to room temperature.
- Grill the kebabs over a charcoal fire; or under a very hot gas or electric grill as described on pp. xiv–xv for 8–10 minutes.
- Turn the skewers every 2 minutes and baste with coconut milk.
- Sprinkle with salt and pepper.
- Arrange the skewers on a serving platter and serve with hot satay peanut sauce on sticky rice.

KASHMIRI CHOPS
TABAK MAAS

Makes 6–8

Kashmir is one of the most beautiful places in India and its cuisine is one of my favourites—rich and aromatic with yogurt and spices such as cardamom, aniseed and saffron. During my childhood we spent our summer holidays with my aunt and uncle in Jammu every year. We hired a cottage which had a kitchen garden and sent our cook a few days ahead to set up the kitchen. My uncle had mastered the art of Kashmiri cuisine and I learned it from him. Tabak maas and Kashmiri shammi kebab are my all-time favourites.

Mutton chops 1 kg
Ghee for deep-frying
Chaat masala powder 1 tsp
Coriander leaves, fresh, chopped 1 tbsp

To cook the chops
Milk ½ cup
Turmeric powder 1 tsp
Aniseed, powdered 1 tsp
Ginger, dried, powdered 1 tsp
Asafoetida powder a pinch
Cinnamon powder 1 tsp
Cloves 2
Salt 2½ tsp

- Wash the chops, trim and drain.
- Cut into portions containing 3–4 chops each, ensuring that the muscles covering the chop bones are not removed. Each piece should be about 5" long and 2" wide.
- Put the ingredients for cooking the chops in a pan with 2¼ cups of water.

- Mix well and add the chops. Bring to a boil on high heat.
- Reduce the heat to medium and simmer for about 30 minutes, till the meat is tender and most of the liquid is absorbed. Remove the chops and set aside.
- Heat the ghee in a kadhai or wok and deep-fry the chops, one piece at a time, till crisp on both sides.
- Drain on kitchen paper.
- Just before serving, put the chops in a pan and place it in an oven preheated to 180ºC for about 5 minutes, to heat through.
- Arrange the chops on a serving platter. Sprinkle chaat masala powder and coriander leaves on top and serve hot with chilli garlic chutney (p. 11) and a radish salad.

MINTED MUTTON CHOPS

Makes 6–8

The aroma of fresh mint with succulent mutton chops is another
Moti Mahal speciality.

Mutton chops 1 kg
Oil, for basting 3 tbsp
Lime juice 1 tbsp

First marinade
Cumin powder 1 tsp
Garam masala powder 2 tsp
White pepper powder 1 tbsp
Salt 4 tsp
Lime juice 5 tsp
White vinegar 1 tbsp

Second marinade
Cream, fresh, whisked 4 tbsp
Yogurt, hung, whisked ¾ cup (p. 5)
Mint chutney 1¼ cups (p. 12)
Maize flour 2 tsp
Papaya, unripe, paste 3 tbsp
Ginger paste 1 tbsp
Garlic paste 1 tbsp
Fenugreek leaves, dried 1 tsp

• Wash the chops, pat dry with paper towels and trim.

First marination
• Combine the ingredients for the first marinade in a bowl and
whisk, till well blended.

- Add the chops and mix well, to ensure that they are completely coated with the marinade.
- Cover and set aside to marinate in the refrigerator for 1 hour.

Second marination
- Mix the cream, yogurt, mint chutney and maize flour in a bowl.
- Add the remaining ingredients for the second marinade and whisk to make a fine paste. Add the marinated chops and mix well, to ensure they are completely coated with the second marinade.
- Cover and set aside to marinate in the refrigerator for 2–3 hours.

For the kebabs
- Remove the meat from the refrigerator and bring to room temperature.
- Thread the meat on to long, thin metal skewers, 1" apart.
- Cook the kebabs in a hot tandoor or grill under a medium-hot gas or electric grill as described on pp. xiv–xv for about 10 minutes.
- Baste with oil, turn the skewers and grill again for another 5 minutes.
- Slip the kebabs off the skewers on to a serving platter.
- Sprinkle lime juice on top and serve hot.

BATTER-FRIED MUTTON CHOP
TUNDEY KEBAB

Makes 2

This is most famously served at the iconic eatery Tundey Miyan in Old Lucknow. Whenever I visit Lucknow, I make it a point to indulge in this mouth-watering delicacy.

As a chef, I must admit that this is a masterpiece and here is my version.

Mutton chops, boneless 200 gm
Milk 1½ cups
Green cardamoms 2
Black cardamom 1
Nutmeg, roughly smashed 1
Cinnamon 1" stick
Whole black pepper 2
Papaya, unripe, paste 3 tbsp
Saffron strands 3-4
Salt 1 tsp
Ghee, melted, for basting 1 tbsp

Batter
Gram flour, roasted 2 ½ tsp
Red chilli powder ½ tsp
Cinnamon powder ⅓ tsp
Green cardamom powder 1 tsp
Cumin powder ⅓ tsp
Black pepper powder ½ tsp
Clove powder ⅓ tsp
Sodium bicarbonate ½ tsp
Salt 1 tsp
Egg, whisked 1
Ginger-garlic paste 1 tbsp
Brown onion paste 1½ tsp (p. 4)
Rose essence ½ tsp

- Wash the chops, pat dry with paper towels and trim. Make small incisions with a knife on both sides of the chops.
- Put the milk in a pan with ½ cup of water over high heat and bring to a boil.
- Reduce heat and add the chops with the remaining ingredients for the chops.
- Cook on low to medium heat, till the chops are tender and the liquid has evaporated. Remove the chops from the pan and let them cool.

Batter
- Whisk the batter ingredients, till smooth.
- Dip the chops in the batter and rub it over the chops to cover completely.

For the kebabs
- Thread the chops on to long, thin metal skewers.
- Grill under a medium-hot gas or electric grill as described on pp. xiv–xv for 5–6 minutes.
- Baste with melted ghee, turn the skewers and grill again for another 6–7 minutes.
- Slip the chops off the skewers on to a serving platter. Serve hot with mint chutney (p. 12) and try it with tortillas (p. 28)—it's divine.

MUTTON CHOPS

Makes 2–3

This is my mother's creation. Whenever she has a party, this is a must on the menu. The succulent, tender, milky chops just melt in your mouth. This recipe is the ultimate if you want to impress someone with your culinary talents.

Single-bone mutton chops 500 gm
Oil, for basting 2 tbsp

Marinade
Ginger paste 2 tbsp
Garlic paste 2 tbsp
Salt 2 tsp

For boiling
Milk 1 litre
Bay leaves 2
Whole black pepper 3
Green cardamoms 3
Cloves 3
Salt 1 tsp

- Wash the chops, pat dry with paper towels and trim.

Marination
- Combine the ingredients for the marinade in a small bowl and rub it on to the chops.
- Set aside for about 30 minutes to marinate.

For the chops
- Put the mutton in a pressure cooker with the ingredients for boiling. Pour in 1 cup of water and mix well.
- Close the cooker and cook on high heat, till the cooker

reaches full pressure. Switch off the heat and wait till the cooker comes to room pressure.
- Open the cooker and remove the chops. Place in a strainer to drain thoroughly.
- Heat the oil in a frying pan. Add the chops and fry on medium heat, till golden-brown on both sides.
- Drain on kitchen paper.
- Serve hot with mint chutney (p. 12) or peanut chutney (p. 15).

BRAISED MUTTON SHANKS IN AUBERGINE WRAPS

Makes 6–8

While interviewing chefs for my restaurants in Saudi Arabia, I came across a really amazing chef who made this kebab for food trials. I loved the aubergine-wrapped kebabs with tomato sauce—I still haven't decided whether it's because of the aubergines or the delicately cooked mutton shanks.

Mutton shoulder, leg or shank, with bone 1 kg
Olive oil 3 tbsp
Onion, large, chopped coarsely 1
Garlic, chopped coarsely 2 cloves
Carrot, medium-sized, chopped coarsely 1
Tomato paste, commercial 2 tbsp
Bay leaves 2
Coriander powder 1 tsp
Green cardamom powder 1 tsp
Whole black pepper 6
Salt 2½ tsp

For the aubergines
Aubergines, large, round 5
Salt 2 tsp
Olive oil or refined oil for shallow-frying

Tomato sauce
Tomato paste 1½ tbsp
Cumin powder 1 tsp
Salt 1 tsp
Black pepper, freshly ground 3/4 tsp

Topping
Tomatoes, medium-sized, sliced 2

Green bell peppers, sliced lengthwise 2
Yellow bell peppers, sliced lengthwise 2
Parsley, fresh, chopped 1 tbsp

- Wash the meat, pat dry with paper towels and trim. Cut it with the bone into 1"-thick chunks.
- Heat the oil in a pan and add the meat. Sauté on medium heat, till the meat is dark brown.
- Add the onion, garlic and carrot and sauté for 2–3 minutes.
- Stir in the tomato paste, bay leaves, spice powders, pepper and 2 cups of water.
- Cover the pan and cook gently on low to medium heat, for about 2 hours, till the meat is tender and leaves the bone. Season with salt and remove from heat.
- Set aside till cool and remove and discard the bones.

For the aubergines

- Peel the aubergines lengthwise in stripes. Cut them lengthwise into ½"-thick slices. Sprinkle salt on both sides and leave for about 15 minutes to drain in a colander.
- Pat with paper towels to remove excess moisture.
- Heat the oil in a frying pan. Shallow-fry the aubergine slices on medium heat for about 2-3 minutes on both sides, till golden-brown.
- Remove with a slotted spoon and drain on paper towels to absorb excess oil. Set aside to cool.

Tomato sauce

- Combine all the sauce ingredients and mix in 2 cups of water.

To assemble the dish

- Place an aubergine slice on a chopping board. Place another at right angles on top of the first slice.
- Spoon some of the cooked meat in the centre, where the 2 slices intersect.
- Fold both aubergine slices over the meat to make a wrap.

- Repeat with the remaining aubergine slices and meat.
- Place the wraps, seam side down, on a lightly greased ovenproof serving platter.
- Lay a slice of tomato and green peppers and yellow on top of each wrap and pierce with a toothpick.
- Pour the sauce around the aubergine wraps.
- Put the dish under a medium-hot grill for 25–30 minutes.
- Serve the kebabs with tomato ketchup and steamed basmati rice.

SYRIAN MEAT LOAF
KEBAB HALABI

Makes 6–8

I have always loved Lebanon—a beautiful country and delicious food. Although halabi kebab is a popular Syrian dish, named after the city of Aleppo (Halab), I discovered it in Lebanon, where it was served with a spicy tomato sauce.

Meat loaf
Beef, ground 1 kg
Oil 1 tbsp
Refined flour 2½ tbsp
Cumin powder ½ tsp
Zhoug 1 tbsp (p. 8)
Salt 1 tsp
Black pepper, freshly ground 1 tsp

Filling
Olive oil ¼ cup
Garlic, minced 1½ tbsp
Salt 2 tsp
Black pepper, freshly ground 1 tsp
Sumac 1 tsp
Cumin powder 1 tsp
Onions, chopped fine 1 cup
Mushrooms, sliced fine 1 cup
Green chillies, chopped fine 50 gm
Coriander leaves, fresh, chopped fine 1 cup
Parsley, fresh, chopped fine 1 cup
Eggs, whisked 3

Meat loaf
- Combine the ingredients for the meat loaf in a bowl.
- Line a 10" loaf tin with aluminium foil. Press the kebab mix

into the tin and make a depression in the centre of the loaf lengthwise, all the way down the length and halfway down the depth.

Filling

- Heat the oil in a large frying pan. Add the garlic and sauté on medium heat till light brown.
- Sprinkle in the salt, pepper, sumac and cumin powder and give it a stir.
- Add the remaining ingredients, except the eggs, and sauté, till the onions turn translucent.
- Spoon the vegetables into the depression in the meat loaf.
- Lightly beat the eggs and pour it over the vegetables.
- Press the sides of the loaf together to cover the vegetables.
- Cover the tin with aluminium foil.
- Place the loaf in an oven preheated to 180ºC and bake for about 30 minutes.
- Serve the loaf hot or cold.

SLICED BEEF KEBABS
BIHARI KEBABS

Makes 2–3

This is a popular dish from Pakistan, even though the name suggests otherwise, as Bihar is a state in India.

Beef 1 kg
Butter, melted, for basting 3 tbsp
Chaat masala powder 1 tsp
Coriander leaves, fresh, chopped 1 tbsp

Marinade
Yogurt, hung, whisked ½ cup (p. 5)
Mustard oil 2 tbsp
Onion, medium-sized, puréed 1
Onion, medium-sized, sliced, fried crisp, crushed 1
Papaya, semi-raw, puréed 1
Red chilli powder 1 tsp
Cumin powder 1 tsp
Coriander powder 2 tsp
Garam masala powder 1 tsp
Salt 2 tsp
Black salt 1 tsp

- Wash the meat, pat dry with paper towels and trim. Cut it into 2"-square slices, ½" thick.
- Put the slices between wet cling-film sheets and flatten them with a mallet or rolling pin into 4"-long, 2"–3" wide pasanda.

Marination
- Combine the ingredients for the marinade in a bowl and whisk, till well blended.
- Add the meat and mix well, to ensure that it is completely coated with the marinade.

- Cover and set aside to marinate in the refrigerator for 7–8 hours.

For the kebabs
- Remove the meat from the refrigerator and bring to room temperature.
- Fold the pasanda and thread them on to long, thin metal skewers. Keep them tightly packed on the skewers.
- Grill the kebabs over a charcoal fire or under a very hot gas or electric grill as described on pp. xiv–xv for 6–7 minutes.
- Baste with melted butter, turn the skewers and grill again for another 6–7 minutes.
- Slip the kebabs off the skewers on to a serving platter.
- Sprinkle chaat masala powder and coriander leaves on top and serve hot with crisp naan (p. 33) and mint chutney (p. 12).

GRILLED BEEF IN A POMEGRANATE MARINADE

KEBAB TORSH

Makes 4

A speciality of northern Iran, this is also called tursh-e-kebab, and comprises grilled beef marinated in a mixture of pomegranate juice, crushed walnuts, parsley, garlic and olive oil.

I learned this recipe from a chef whom I interviewed while I was in Doha, Qatar, to open my restaurant in the city. He made kebab torsh during his trials and as I observed him I noted down the recipe. The next day I decided to repeat the recipe, but could not slice the fillets with the same finesse as the chef. I could succeed only after several attempts. So here is my version of the recipe.

Fillet of beef, kept whole 750 gm
Oil, for basting 3 tbsp

Marinade
Onion, chopped roughly 1
Pomegranate juice, fresh 1 cup
Parsley, fresh, chopped 1 tsp
Walnuts, ground fine to a paste 1 cup
Green cardamom powder ½ tsp
Salt 2 tsp
Black pepper, freshly ground 1 tsp

- Wash the fillet, trim and drain thoroughly.
- Slice the fillet lengthwise into 2 long strips, then cut it breadthwise into 10–12 rectangles. Lay a rectangle on a wet chopping board. Hold the meat down with the palm of your hand. Using a very sharp knife, make a slit along the length of the rectangle one-third of the way down the breadth. Do not cut all the way across; leave 1" uncut.
- Turn the rectangle over and repeat on the other side. There

should be 2 slits dividing the rectangle into 3 pieces, but without separating them.
- Unfold to make 1 long slice of meat.
- Repeat with the rest of the meat.

Marination
- Purée the onion with 1 tbsp of water in a blender to make a smooth paste. Strain the purée through a fine-meshed strainer into a bowl. Discard the residue.
- Add the remaining ingredients for the marinade to the bowl and whisk, till well blended.
- Add the meat and mix well, to ensure that it is completely coated with the marinade.
- Cover and set aside to marinate in the refrigerator for 24 hours.

For the kebabs
- Remove the meat from the refrigerator and bring to room temperature.
- Wipe the meat of excess marinade with paper towels.
- Thread each piece on to a skewer, along the length of the slice, so that the slice remains flat.
- Grill the kebabs under a medium-hot gas or electric grill as described on pp. xiv–xv for 7–8 minutes.
- Baste with oil, turn the skewers and grill again for another 7–8 minutes.
- Slip the kebabs off the skewers on to a serving platter.
- Serve with a rice pulao and lime wedges.

GREEK SAUSAGES
SHEFTALIA

Makes 30 sheftalia

In 2010, I was invited by Le Cordon Bleu in Paris to demonstrate Indian cuisine to the students. While I had gone to teach at the institute, in return I learned the recipe for this sheftalia from a Greek student.

Sheftalia kebab is a traditional Greek-Cypriot sausage made without the sausage casing. It normally consists of pork or mutton, wrapped in pork caul fat, which is used instead of sausage casing. No basting is required as the caul has its own fat content.

Pork, shoulder, ground 500 gm
Mutton, shoulder or leg, ground 500 gm
Pork fatback, without rind, chopped fine 100 gm
Garlic paste ½ tsp
Parsley, fresh, chopped fine ½ cup
Cumin powder ½ tsp
Salt 2 tsp
Black pepper, freshly ground 2 tsp
Pork caul fat 150 gm
Onion, sliced 1
Lime, cut into wedges 1

- Combine all the ingredients, except the caul fat, in a bowl. Mix till they blend well.
- Shape the kebab mix into 30 oval sausages. Flatten them slightly.
- Carefully unfold the caul fat and stretch it out over the work surface. Cut it into 30 squares, 4"–5" wide.
- Place a sausage on each square and wrap it into a neat little package, shaping it with the palms of your hand.
- Put the sheftalia on a plate, cover and place in the refrigerator overnight.

For the sheftalia

- Remove the sheftalia from the refrigerator and bring to room temperature.
- Thread the sheftalia on to long, thin metal skewers, 1" apart.
- Grill the sheftalia under a very hot gas or electric grill as described on pp. xiv–xv for 20–30 minutes, turning them occasionally, till golden-brown.
- I recommend serving this sausage with Italian bread (p. 26), onion slices, lime wedges and chilli garlic chutney (p. 11).

ĆEVAPČIĆI OR ČEVAPI

Makes 6–8

I love this dish because of its unique combination of beef, mutton and pork, with a hint of garlic and coriander. During my kebab trail, I visited Bosnia where I was invited for dinner by a friend whom I urged to cook the local kebabs. Ćevapčići was the obvious choice on the menu that day.

A dish of grilled minced meat, it is popular in several Balkan countries and is considered a national dish in Bosnia and Serbia.

Beef, lean, ground 500 gm
Mutton, ground 250 gm
Pork, ground 250 gm
Garlic, minced fine 5 cloves
Red chilli powder 1 tsp
Coriander powder ½ tsp
Black pepper, freshly ground 2 tsp
Salt 2½ tsp
Club soda ½ cup
Egg white, whisked 1
Parsley, fresh, chopped 2 tbsp

- Combine the ground meat with the garlic, spice powders and salt.
- Mix with your hands, till it is well blended.
- Pour in the club soda gradually, mixing between each addition, till it is absorbed.
- Add the whisked egg white and mix again, till it blends well.
- Shape the kebab mix into 4" long, ¾" thick oval kebabs and arrange on a plate.
- Cover and place in the refrigerator for 1 hour.

- Remove the kebabs from the refrigerator and bring to room temperature.
- Grill the kebabs under a medium-hot gas or electric grill as described on pp. xiv–xv for about 4–5 minutes on each side.
- Slip the kebabs off the skewers on to a serving platter.
- Sprinkle parsley on top and serve hot with pita bread (p. 24) and a garlic dip.

CHICKEN KEBABS IN A CRISP COATING
MURGH GILAFI KEBAB

Makes 3–4

Gilafi in Urdu means to cover. So, as the name suggests, this kebab involves a cover-up: a cover-up of special spices and condiments. You are about to learn one of Pakistan's most famous recipes.

Chicken, boneless, without skin, minced 700 gm
Egg yolks, whisked 4
Coriander leaves, fresh, chopped fine 3 tsp
Mint leaves, fresh, chopped 2 tsp
Green chillies, chopped fine 2 tsp
Ginger, chopped fine 1 tsp
Brown onion paste 3 tbsp (p. 4)
Lime juice 2 tsp
Olive oil 3 tbsp
Pomegranate seeds, dried, crushed 1 tsp
Red chilli powder 1 tsp
Green cardamom powder 1 tsp
Cumin seeds, roasted 1 tsp
Salt 1½ tsp
Butter, melted, for basting 3 tbsp

For coating
Egg yolks, whisked 5
Coriander leaves, fresh, chopped fine 2 tbsp
Mint leaves, fresh, chopped fine 2 tbsp

- Combine the ingredients for the kebab in a bowl and mix thoroughly.
- Combine the coating ingredients in another bowl and mix well.
- Wet your hands and a few long, thick metal skewers.
- Roll the kebab mix into 4 balls and thread them on to the skewers. Shape the balls into 2" long kebabs along the length of the skewers, 1" apart.
- Brush the kebabs with the coating mix.

For the kebabs
- Cook the kebabs in a medium hot tandoor or grill under a very hot gas or electric grill as described on pp. xiv–xv for 5–6 minutes.
- Baste with melted butter, turn the skewers and grill again for another 4–5 minutes.
- Slip the kebabs off the skewers on to a serving platter and serve hot with mint chutney (p. 12).

PEANUT-FLAVOURED CHICKEN KEBABS

Makes 3–4

This is one of my own inventions as I love peanuts: anything to do with peanuts, whether it's peanut chocolate, peanut butter or peanut masala. I invented this one for my own taste buds and hope you enjoy my spectacular creation.

Chicken, boneless, without skin, minced 600 gm

First marinade
Ginger paste 1 tsp
Garlic paste 1 tsp
Lime juice 2 tsp
Red chilli powder ¼ tsp
Salt 2 tsp
Oil, for basting 2 tbsp
Parsley, fresh, chopped 2 tsp

Second marinade
Cheese spread, commercial 4 tsp
Peanut butter 2 tsp
Cream, fresh, whisked 2 tsp
Green chillies, chopped fine 1 tsp
Coriander leaves, fresh, chopped fine 2 tsp
White pepper, freshly ground 1 tsp
Ginger, dried, powdered 1 tsp
Green cardamom powder 1 tsp
Cinnamon powder ¼ tsp

- Put the chicken mince in a large bowl.

First marination
- Combine the ingredients for the first marinade in a small bowl.

- Add it to the chicken mince and stir, till the ingredients are well blended.
- Cover and set aside to marinate in the refrigerator for about 30 minutes.

Second marination
- Mix the cheese with the remaining ingredients for the second marinade and whisk till well blended.
- Add the marinated chicken and mix well, to ensure that it is completely coated with the second marinade.
- Cover and set aside to marinate in the refrigerator for 6–7 hours.

For the kebabs
- Remove the chicken from the refrigerator and bring to room temperature.
- Wet your hands and a few long, thick metal skewers.
- Roll the kebab mix into small balls and thread them on to the skewers. Shape the balls into 2" long kebabs along the length of the skewers, 1" apart.
- Grill the kebabs under a medium-hot gas or electric grill as described on pp. xiv–xv for 7–8 minutes.
- Baste with oil, turn the skewers and grill again for another 3–4 minutes.
- Slip the kebabs off the skewers on to a serving platter.
- Serve hot with mint chutney (p. 12) and a salad.

CHICKEN TIKKA

Make 2

Chicken tikka is one of the most common dishes available in almost all North Indian restaurants. This one is a bestseller in the Moti Mahal menu. The trick is not to overcook the chicken tikka or as a matter of fact any kebab, in order to make it succulent and juicy .

Chicken, boneless, without skin 350 gm
Butter, melted, for basting 3 tbsp

First marinade
Ginger paste 1 tsp
Garlic paste 1 tsp
Lime juice 2 tbsp
Salt 1 tsp

Second marinade
Yogurt, hung, whisked ¼ cup (p. 5)
Malt vinegar 1 tbsp
Fenugreek leaves, dried 1 tsp
Red degi chilli powder 2 tsp
Cumin powder 1½ tsp
Chaat masala powder 1 tsp
Meat masala, commercial 1 tsp
Garam masala powder 1½ tsp
Black salt 1 tsp

• Wash the chicken and pat dry with paper towels. Cut it into 2" cubes.

First marination
• Combine the ingredients for the first marinade in a bowl and whisk, till they blend well.

- Add the chicken and rub in the marinade so that it is completely coated.
- Cover and set aside to marinate in the refrigerator for about 1 hour.

Second marination
- Combine the ingredients for the second marinade in another bowl and whisk, till they blend well.
- Add the marinated chicken and mix well, to ensure that it is completely coated with the second marinade.
- Cover and set aside to marinate in the refrigerator for 3–4 hours.

For the tikkas
- Remove the chicken from the refrigerator and bring to room temperature.
- Thread the chicken on to long, thin metal skewers, 1" apart.
- Cook the kebabs in a medium-hot tandoor; or grill over a charcoal fire; or under a very hot gas or electric grill as described on pp. xiv–xv for 6–7 minutes.
- Baste with melted butter, turn the skewers and grill again for another 3–4 minutes.
- Slip the kebabs off the skewers on to a serving platter and serve hot with mint chutney (p. 12).

CHICKEN KEBABS

RAJASTHANI MURGH BURRAH

Makes 2–3

Succulent chicken kebabs from the princely state of Rajasthan.
This is a special kebab preparation which I learnt from one of the
royal chefs in Jodhpur.

Chicken, boneless, without skin 500 gm
Refined oil, for basting 2 tbsp
Coriander leaves, fresh, chopped 1 tbsp

First marinade
Ginger paste 1 tsp
Garlic paste 1 tsp
Red chilli powder 1 tsp
Salt 1 tsp
Lime juice 1 tsp
Mustard oil 4 tsp

Second marinade
Yogurt, hung, whisked 8 tsp (p. 5)
Salt 2 tsp
Red chilli powder 2 tsp
Cumin powder ½ tsp
Fenugreek seeds, powdered 1 tsp
Garam masala powder 1 tsp
Cinnamon powder 1 tsp
Mustard oil 4 tsp

- Wash the chicken and pat dry with paper towels. Cut it into 8
  pieces.

First marination

- Combine the ingredients for the first marinade in a bowl and whisk, till they blend well.
- Add the chicken and mix well, to ensure that it is completely coated with the marinade.
- Cover and set aside to marinate in the refrigerator for about 1 hour.

Second marination

- Whisk the yogurt in a deep bowl. Add the remaining ingredients for the second marinade and whisk, till they blend well.
- Add the marinated chicken and mix well, to ensure that it is completely coated with the second marinade.
- Cover and set aside to marinate in the refrigerator for 7–8 hours.

For the kebabs

- Remove the chicken from the refrigerator and bring to room temperature.
- Thread the chicken on to long, thin metal skewers, 1" apart.
- Grill the kebabs under a very hot gas or electric grill as described on pp. xiv–xv for 7–8 minutes.
- Baste with oil, turn the skewers and grill again for another 3–4 minutes.
- Slip the kebabs off the skewers on to a serving platter. Sprinkle coriander leaves on top and serve hot with mint chutney (p. 12).

SAFFRON CHICKEN KEBABS

Makes 2–3

Saffron is the most expensive spice in the world and makes this kebab exquisite.

Chicken, boneless, without skin 500 gm
Oil for shallow-frying
Coriander leaves, fresh, chopped 1 tsp

Marinade
Processed Cheddar cheese 6 tsp
Egg yolks, whisked 2
Cream, fresh, whisked 4 tbsp
Garlic paste 1 tsp
Ginger paste 1 tsp
Gram flour, roasted 4 tsp
Coriander powder 1 tsp
White pepper powder, freshly ground 1 tsp
Green cardamom powder ½ tsp
Saffron strands 1 tbsp
Salt 2 tsp

- Wash the chicken and pat dry with paper towels. Cut it into 16 pieces.

Marination
- Mash the cheese in a deep bowl.
- Add the remaining ingredients for the marinade, except the salt.
- Whisk till the marinade is well blended.
- Taste and add salt.
- Add the chicken and mix well, to ensure that it is completely coated with the marinade.

- Cover and set aside to marinate in the refrigerator for 2–3 hours.

For the kebabs
- Remove the chicken from the refrigerator and bring to room temperature.
- Soak 4 bamboo skewers in water for about 20 minutes and drain.
- Thread 4 chicken pieces on to each skewer.
- Heat the oil in a frying pan.
- Put the skewers into the pan and fry, turning the skewers, till the chicken is golden on all sides and cooked through.
- Arrange the skewers on a serving platter. Sprinkle coriander leaves on top and serve hot mint chutney (p. 12) and any salad of your choice.

HYDERABADI CHICKEN KEBABS

Makes 2–3

A few years ago, when I was in Hyderabad for the opening of one of my Moti Mahal outlets, I invited a member of the Nawab's family to the restaurant. He was a great chef himself, and this recipe was his gift to me.

Chicken breast, boneless, without skin 500 gm
Oil, for basting 2 tbsp
Onion, sliced 1

First marinade
Ginger paste 1 tsp
Garlic paste 1 tsp
Lime juice ½ tsp
Salt 1 tsp
White pepper powder 1½ tsp

Second marinade
Cheese spread, commercial 4 tbsp
Egg whites, whisked 2
Ginger paste 1 tsp
Garlic paste 1 tsp
Cream, fresh, whisked 6 tbsp
Tamarind pulp 4 tsp
White pepper powder 2 tsp
Green cardamom powder 1 tsp
Green chillies, chopped fine 1 tsp
Cumin seeds 1 tsp
Almonds, chopped fine 4 tsp
Saffron strands 1 tsp
Salt 1 tsp

- Wash the chicken and pat dry with paper towels. Cut it into 12 pieces.

First marination

- Combine the ingredients for the first marinade in a bowl and whisk, till they blend well.
- Add the chicken and mix well, to ensure that the pieces are completely coated with the marinade.
- Cover and set aside to marinate in the refrigerator for about 30 minutes.

Second marination

- Mash the cheese in a deep bowl.
- Add the egg whites, ginger paste and garlic paste and whisk, till they blend well.
- Add the remaining ingredients for the second marinade, except the salt. Mix well.
- Taste and add salt. Whisk till well blended
- Add the marinated chicken and mix well, to ensure that it is completely coated with the second marinade.
- Cover and set aside to marinate in the refrigerator for 3–4 hours.

For the kebabs

- Remove the chicken from the refrigerator and bring to room temperature.
- Thread the chicken on to long, thin metal skewers, 1" apart.
- Grill the kebabs under a very hot gas or electric grill as described on pp. xiv–xv for 7–8 minutes.
- Baste with oil, turn the skewers and grill again for another 3–4 minutes.
- Slip the kebabs off the skewers on to a serving platter. Sprinkle onion slices on top and serve hot with mint chutney (p. 12).

KANDAHARI CHICKEN KEBABS

Makes 2–3

Kandahar is famous for its pomegranates, and since this recipe uses fresh pomegranate, which gives its unique sweet and tangy taste to the kebabs, I called it Kandahari chicken kebabs.

Chicken legs, boneless, without skin 500 gm
Ghee, melted, for basting 3 tbsp
Pomegranate seeds, fresh 2 tsp
Parsley, fresh, chopped 1 tbsp

First marinade
Ginger paste 1 tsp
Garlic paste 1 tsp
Lime juice ½ tsp
Pomegranate juice, fresh 4 tsp

Second marinade
Yogurt, hung, whisked 6 tbsp (p. 5)
Ginger paste 1 tsp
Garlic paste 1 tsp
Pomegranate juice, fresh 4 tsp
Pomegranate seeds, fresh, crushed 6 tsp
Fenugreek seeds, powdered 1 tsp
Red chilli paste 1 tsp
Cumin powder 1 tsp
Oil 2 tsp
Salt 2 tsp

- Wash the chicken and pat dry with paper towels. Cut it into 8 pieces.

First marination
- Combine the ingredients for the first marinade in a bowl and whisk, till they blend well.

- Add the chicken and mix well, to ensure that it is completely coated with the marinade.
- Cover and set aside to marinate in the refrigerator for about 30 minutes.

Second marination
- Whisk the yogurt in a deep bowl. Add the remaining ingredients for the second marinade, in the order given and whisk, till they blend well.
- Add the marinated chicken and mix well, to ensure that it is completely coated with the second marinade.
- Cover and set aside to marinate in the refrigerator for 6–8 hours.

For the kebabs
- Remove the chicken from the refrigerator and bring to room temperature.
- Thread the chicken on to long, thin metal skewers, 1" apart.
- Grill the kebabs under a very hot gas *or* electric grill as described on pp. xiv–xv for 7–8 minutes.
- Baste with melted ghee, turn the skewers and grill again for another 3–4 minutes.
- Slip the kebabs off the skewers on to a serving platter. Sprinkle pomegranate seeds and parsley on top and serve hot with mint chutney (p. 12).

GARLIC CHICKEN KEBABS

Makes 2

This is again a very popular kebab on the Moti Mahal menu. We marinate it with spinach and garlic paste to impart a garlicky flavour and the appetizing green colour. A must in my parties, it tastes great with sour cream or mint chutney (p. 12).

Chicken, boneless, without skin 350 gm
Butter, melted, for basting 2 tbsp

First marinade
Ginger-garlic paste 1 tsp
Lime juice 2 tbsp
Salt 1½ tsp

Second marinade
Spinach, chopped ½ tbsp
Salt 1½ tsp
Garlic paste 1 tsp
Green chillies, seeded 2–3
Egg, whisked 1
Yogurt, hung, whisked ½ cup (p. 5)
Cashew nut and cheese paste ½ cup (p. 6)
Cream, fresh, whisked 5 tsp
Coriander powder ½ tsp
White pepper, freshly ground ¾ tsp
Green cardamom powder ¾ tsp

- Wash the chicken and pat dry with paper towels. Cut it into 2" cubes.

First marination
- Combine the ingredients for the first marinade in a bowl and whisk, till they blend well.

- Add the chicken and rub in the marinade so that it is completely coated.
- Cover and set aside to marinate in the refrigerator for about 1 hour.
- How do you boil ½ tbsp of spinach?

Second marination
- Boil the spinach with a pinch of salt for 30 seconds. Drain thoroughly and grind to a paste with the remaining salt and garlic paste and green chillies.
- Transfer to a bowl and mix in the remaining ingredients for the second marinade.
- Add the marinated chicken and mix well, to ensure that it is completely coated with the second marinade.
- Cover and set aside to marinate in the refrigerator for 3–4 hours.

For the kebabs
- Remove the chicken from the refrigerator and bring to room temperature.
- Thread the chicken on to long, thin metal skewers, 1" apart.
- Cook the kebabs in a medium-hot tandoor; or grill over a charcoal fire as described on pp. xiv–xv for 6–7 minutes.
- Baste with melted butter, turn the skewers and grill again for another 3–4 minutes.
- Slip the kebabs off the skewers on to a serving platter and serve hot with mint chutney (p. 12).

TURKISH CHICKEN SHISH KEBAB

Makes 3–4

I was in Turkey on a research trip for this book. On asking the concierge of the hotel about some interesting restaurants in Istanbul, he recommended that I go to a place near the old fish market, which has a line of restaurants. I got friendly with a restaurateur who taught me this recipe and whenever I serve these kebabs they are always praised.

Chicken breasts, boneless, without skin, 100 gm each, 4
Olive oil, for basting 3 tbsp
Sumac ½ tsp
Parsley, fresh, chopped 1 tsp

Marinade
Yogurt, hung, whisked 1 cup (p. 5)
Onion, grated ½ cup
Garlic, minced 3 cloves
Lime juice 1 tbsp
Olive oil 3 tbsp
Red chilli powder ½ tsp
Cumin powder 1 tsp
Green cardamom powder 1 tsp
White pepper, freshly ground ½ tsp
Black pepper, freshly ground 1 tsp
Sugar ¼ tsp
Salt 1 tsp

- Wash the chicken and pat dry with paper towels.

Marination
- Combine the ingredients for the marinade in a bowl and whisk, till well blended.

- Add the chicken and mix well, to ensure that it is completely coated with the marinade.
- Cover and set aside to marinate in the refrigerator overnight.

For the kebabs
- Remove the chicken from the refrigerator and bring to room temperature.
- Thread the chicken on to long, thin metal skewers, 1" apart.
- Grill the kebabs under a very hot gas or electric grill as described on pp. xiv–xv for 6–8 minutes.
- Baste with olive oil, turn the skewers and grill again for another 3–4 minutes.
- Slip the kebabs off the skewers on to a serving platter, sprinkle sumac and parsley on top and serve hot with a salad and Moroccan flatbread (p. 30).

BANNO KEBAB

Makes 2

A popular kebab recipe from Pakistan. I vividly remember a senior Hindu chef in Moti Mahal during my youth. He too had migrated to India during the Partition in 1947 and he would cook this dish on very special occasions.

Chicken, boneless, without skin 350 gm
Butter, melted 1½ tbsp
Chaat masala powder 1½ tsp
Coriander leaves, fresh, chopped 1 tbsp

First marinade
Ginger-garlic paste 1 tbsp
Lime juice 1 tsp
Salt 1½ tsp

Second marinade
Oil 2 tbsp
Ginger, chopped ½ tsp
Garlic, chopped ½ tsp
Green chillies, chopped ½ tsp
Gram flour 1 tbsp
Turmeric powder ¼ tsp
Yellow chilli powder ½ tsp
Cumin powder ¼ tsp
Milk 100 ml
Yogurt, hung, whisked 2½ tbsp (p. 5)
Lime juice 1 tsp
Fenugreek leaves, dried ½ tsp
Green cardamom powder ¼ tsp

Coating
Egg, whisked 1
Coriander leaves, fresh, chopped ½ tsp
Butter, melted 1 tbsp
Cream, fresh 1 tbsp
Chaat masala powder 1½ tsp
A few saffron strands, dissolved in 2 tsp water
Cashew nuts, chopped 1½ tbsp

- Wash the chicken and pat dry with paper towels. Cut it in 2"
  cubes.

First marination
- Combine the ingredients for the marinade in a bowl and mix
  well.
- Add the chicken and rub in the marinade so that it is
  completely coated.
- Cover and set aside to marinate in the refrigerator for about
  30 minutes.

Second marination
- Heat the oil in a pan and add the ginger, garlic and green
  chillies. Sauté on low to medium heat for 1 minute.
- Add the gram flour and stir on low heat, till the oil separates.
- Sprinkle in the spice powders and cook for a few seconds.
- Pour in the milk and stir, till the contents of the pan blend
  well.
- Remove the pan from heat and pour the contents into a
  bowl.
- Add the remaining ingredients for the second marinade and
  whisk well.
- Add the marinated chicken pieces and mix well, to ensure that
  the pieces are completely coated with the second marinade.
- Cover and set aside to marinate in the refrigerator for 4–5
  hours

For the kebabs

- Remove the chicken from the refrigerator and bring to room temperature.
- Thread the chicken on to long, thin metal skewers, 1" apart.
- Grill the kebabs under a medium-hot gas or electric grill as described on pp. xiv–xv for 10–12 minutes.
- Remove the skewers from the grill and raise the heat to very high.
- Whisk the coating ingredients together in a bowl.
- Brush the partially cooked chicken pieces with the coating.
- Return the skewers to the hot grill and grill, till the egg is set.
- Remove the skewers from the oven and brush the chicken with melted butter.
- Slip the chicken off the skewers on to a serving platter.
- Sprinkle chaat masala powder and coriander leaves on top and serve hot with crisp naan (p. 33).

GINGER CHICKEN KEBABS

Makes 6–8

The subtle flavour of ginger and aromatic spices makes this kebab special. Whenever we want to have a light supper at home this is the one my wife Sonal makes. Have it with pickled onion and green chutney—you can never go wrong with this.

Chicken breasts, boneless, without skin 1 kg
Ginger, julienned 2 tsp
Coriander leaves, fresh, chopped 2 tsp

First marinade
Green chilli paste 1 tbsp
Ginger paste 4 tbsp
Malt vinegar 4 tsp
Lime juice 1 tbsp
White pepper powder 2 tsp
Salt 2½ tsp

Second marinade
Yogurt, hung, whisked 1 cup (p. 5)
Cream, fresh, whisked 4 tbsp
Coriander powder 1 tsp

- Wash the chicken and pat dry with paper towels. Cut it into 2" cubes.

First marination
- Combine the ingredients for the first marinade in a bowl and whisk, till they blend well.
- Add the chicken and mix well, to ensure that it is completely coated with the marinade.
- Cover and set aside to marinate in the refrigerator for about 30 minutes.

Second marination

- Combine the ingredients for the second marinade in a bowl and whisk, till they blend well.
- Add the marinated chicken and mix well, to ensure that it is completely coated with the second marinade.
- Cover and set aside to marinate in the refrigerator for about 1 hour.

For the kebabs

- Remove the chicken from the refrigerator and bring to room temperature.
- Thread the chicken on to long, thin metal skewers, 1" apart.
- Grill the kebabs over a charcoal fire; or under a medium-hot gas or electric grill as described on pp. xiv–xv for 6–7 minutes.
- Baste with the leftover marinade, turn the skewers and grill again for another 3–4 minutes.
- Slip the kebabs off the skewers on to a serving platter.
- Sprinkle the julienned ginger and coriander leaves on top and serve hot.

CHICKEN AND GRAM KEBABS

Makes 2–3

I love this kebab, taught to me by my cousin. The flavour of roasted gram flour with the selected spices makes it a super appetizer. Serve with garlic flatbread.

Chicken breast, boneless, without skin 500 gm
Oil, for basting 4 tbsp
Chaat masala powder ½ tsp
Onion, sliced 1

Marinade
Gram flour 3 tsp
Yogurt, hung, whisked 1 cup (p. 5)
Green chillies, chopped fine 2
Ginger paste 1 tsp
Garlic paste 1 tsp
Lime juice 1 tsp
Olive oil 1 tbsp
Turmeric powder ½ tsp
Red chilli powder 1 tsp
Cumin powder 1 tsp
Coriander powder ½ tsp
Garam masala powder 1 tsp
Salt 2 tsp

- Wash the chicken and pat dry with paper towels. Cut it into 2" cubes.

Marination
- Put a frying pan on low heat and add the gram flour. Roast for about 5 minutes, tossing all the while, till the colour changes to golden-brown.
- Remove from heat and let it cool.

- Transfer the roasted gram flour to a bowl and stir in the remaining ingredients for the marinade. Whisk, till well blended.
- Add the chicken and mix well, to ensure that it is completely coated with the marinade.
- Cover and set aside to marinate in the refrigerator for 6–8 hours.

For the kebabs
- Remove the chicken from the refrigerator and bring to room temperature.
- Thread the chicken on to long, thin metal skewers, 1" apart.
- Grill the kebabs under a very hot gas or electric grill as described on pp. xiv–xv for 5–6 minutes.
- Baste with oil, turn the skewers and grill again for another 5–6 minutes or till the chicken is tender.
- Slip the kebabs off the skewers on to a serving platter.
- Sprinkle chaat masala powder on top and serve hot with onion slices, mint chutney (p. 12) and garlic flatbread (p. 31).

GARDEN GREEN
CHICKEN TIKKA

Makes 2–3

This green kebab gets its colour from the spinach and coriander leaves. It's a great-looking appetizer. Try serving it with crisp Turkish lavash (p. 29).

Chicken boneless, without skin 750 gm
Butter, melted, for basting 3 tbsp
Parsley, fresh, chopped 1 tsp

First marinade
Ginger paste ½ tsp
Garlic paste ½ tsp
Oil 2 tbsp
Lime juice 1 tbsp
White vinegar ½ tsp
White pepper 1 tsp
Salt 1½ tsp

Second marinade
Coriander leaves, fresh 200 gm
Mint leaves, fresh 80 gm
Spinach, boiled 50 gm
Green chillies, seeded 2
Yogurt, hung, whisked ½ cup (p. 5)
Ginger paste ½ tsp
Garlic paste ½ tsp
Lime juice 2 tbsp
Mustard oil 5 tbsp
Coriander powder 1 tsp
Garam masala powder 1 tsp

- Wash the chicken and pat dry with paper towels. Cut it into 2" cubes.

First marination
- Combine the ingredients for the first marinade in a bowl and whisk, till they blend well.
- Add the chicken and rub in the marinade so that it is completely coated.
- Cover and set aside to marinate in the refrigerator for about 2 hours.

Second marination
- Grind the coriander leaves, mint leaves, spinach and green chillies to make a fine paste. Transfer to another bowl.
- Add the remaining ingredients for the second marinade and whisk, till they blend well.
- Add the marinated chicken and mix well, to ensure that it is completely coated with the second marinade.
- Cover and set aside to marinate in the refrigerator for 1 hour.

For the tikkas
- Remove the chicken from the refrigerator and bring to room temperature.
- Thread the chicken on to long, thin metal skewers, 1" apart.
- Cook the kebabs in a medium-hot tandoor; or grill over a charcoal fire; or under a very hot gas or electric grill as described on pp. xiv–xv for 5–6 minutes.
- Baste with melted butter, turn the skewers and grill again for another 3–4 minutes.
- Slip the chicken off the skewers on to a serving platter. Sprinkle parsley on top and serve hot with Turkish lavash (p. 29) and mint chutney (p. 12) or sesame tomato chutney (p. 14).

MINTED CHICKEN KEBABS

Makes 2

This kebab is a great snack. I normally serve it when we have guests over for a drink, as it is easy to make and mint brings out the flavour of chicken.

Chicken, boneless, without skin 350 gm
Butter, melted, for basting 2 tbsp

First marinade
Ginger-garlic paste 1 tbsp
Lime juice 2 tbsp
Salt 1 tsp

Second marinade
Egg, whisked 1
Mint leaves, fresh, chopped 3 tbsp
Puréed spinach 1 tbsp
Green cardamom powder ½ tsp
White pepper, freshly ground 1 tsp

- Wash the chicken and pat dry with paper towels. Cut it into 2" cubes.

First marination
- Combine the ingredients for the first marinade in a bowl and whisk, till they blend well.
- Add the chicken and rub in the marinade so that it is completely coated.
- Cover and set aside to marinate in the refrigerator for about 1 hour.

Second marination
- Combine the ingredients for the second marinade in a bowl and whisk, till they blend well.

- Add the marinated chicken and mix well, to ensure that it is completely coated with the second marinade.
- Cover and set aside to marinate in the refrigerator for 3–4 hours.

For the kebabs
- Remove the chicken from the refrigerator and bring to room temperature.
- Thread the chicken on to long, thin metal skewers, 1" apart.
- Cook the kebabs in a medium-hot tandoor or grill under a very hot gas or electric grill as described on pp. xiv–xv for 6–7 minutes.
- Baste with melted butter, turn the skewers and grill again for another 3–4 minutes.
- Slip the kebabs off the skewers on to a serving platter and serve hot with mint chutney (p. 12).

DUM KA MURGH KEBAB

Makes 2–3

Nowadays slow cooking ovens are the latest fad all over the world. However, this is an ancient Indian cooking technique used in royal kitchens to retain the flavours and aromas of the spices in the dish.

This is one of my special creations and always a great hit at parties.

Chicken, boneless, without skin 500 gm
Oil, for frying ½ cup
Onion, large, sliced 1
Coriander leaves, fresh, chopped 1 tbsp

Marinade
Yogurt, hung, whisked 4 tbsp (p. 5)
Ginger paste 1 tsp
Garlic paste 1 tsp
Jaggery, grated 1 tsp
Sesame seeds 1 tsp
Soy sauce 1 tsp
Dry sherry 2 tbsp
Cinnamon powder ¼ tsp
Black pepper, coarsely crushed 1 tsp
Salt 2 tsp

- Wash the chicken and pat dry with paper towels. Cut it into 8 pieces.

Marination
- Whisk the yogurt in a deep bowl. Add the remaining ingredients for the marinade in the order given, and whisk till they blend well.

- Add the chicken and mix well, to ensure that it is completely coated with the marinade.
- Cover and set aside to marinate in the refrigerator for 8–9 hours.

For the kebabs
- Heat the oil in a heavy-bottomed pan.
- Add the chicken pieces and cook on very low heat. Keep turning the chicken occasionally, basting with oil, till tender and crisp.
- Remove from heat and drain on kitchen paper.
- Transfer to a serving platter and sprinkle onion slices and coriander leaves on top. Serve immediately with Italian flatbread (p. 26).

NIGELLA CHICKEN KEBABS

Makes 3–4

Nigella seeds, *kalaunji* in Hindi, and sometimes mistakenly called onion seeds, are used as a spice in Indian and Middle Eastern cuisines. Roasted nigella seeds flavour curries, vegetables and pulses. In this recipe, they impart a special flavour to the kebab as their taste is a combination of onion, black pepper and oregano, and with a slight hint of bitterness like mustard seeds.

Chicken, boneless, without skin, minced 700 gm
Processed Cheddar cheese, grated 4 tsp
Cashew nut paste 2 tbsp
Ginger paste 1 tsp
Garlic paste 1 tsp
Onion, small, chopped fine 1
Green chilli, chopped fine 1
Red chilli powder ½ tsp
Chaat masala powder 1 tsp
Green cardamom powder 1 tsp
Black pepper powder ½ tsp
Lime juice 1 tsp
Egg yolks, whisked 2
Salt 1½ tsp
Nigella seeds 2 tsp
Mustard seeds 1 tsp
Sesame seeds 1 tsp
Coriander leaves, fresh, chopped fine 1 tsp
Butter, melted, for basting 3 tbsp

- Put the chicken mince, cashew nut paste, cheese, ginger paste and garlic paste in a bowl and mix, till they blend well.
- Stir in the onion, green chilli, spice powders, lime juice, egg yolks and salt.
- Mix well with your hands.

- Heat the whole spices on a dry tava or griddle for a few seconds and add them to the bowl with the coriander leaves.
- Mix and knead, till ingredients are well distributed.
- Wet your hands and a few long, thick metal skewers.
- Roll the kebab mix into 12 small balls and thread them on to the skewers. Shape the balls into small sausage-shaped kebabs along the length of the skewers, 1" apart.

For the kebabs
- Cook the kebabs in a medium-hot tandoor; or grill under a very hot gas or electric grill as described on pp. xiv–xv for 5–6 minutes.
- Baste with melted butter, turn the skewers and grill again for another 4–5 minutes.
- Slip the kebabs off the skewers on to a serving platter and serve hot with mint chutney (p. 12) and Turkish lavash (p. 29).

THAI CHICKEN KEBABS

Makes 8

This recipe was inspired by my love for Thai food. I find the flavour of lemon grass irresistible, so I thought of infusing it in chicken kebabs with just a hint of peanut butter.

Chicken breast, boneless, without skin 1 kg
Oil, for basting 3 tbsp

Marinade
Peanut butter 150 gm
Red chilli paste 4 tbsp
Garlic, chopped fine 4 cloves
Ginger, grated 2 tsp
Lemon grass stalks, finely chopped 6
Soy sauce ¼ cup
Cider vinegar 2 tbsp
Red chilli powder ½ tsp
Sugar 1 tsp
Salt 3 tsp

- Wash the chicken and pat dry with paper towels. Cut it into 1" cubes.

Marination
- Put the peanut butter into a large bowl. Gradually add ½ cup of hot water and mix, till it blends well.
- Add the remaining ingredients for the marinade and mix well.
- Add the chicken and mix well, to ensure that it is completely coated with the marinade.
- Cover and refrigerate overnight, turning the pieces occasionally.

For the kebabs
- Remove the chicken from the refrigerator and bring to room temperature.
- Thread the chicken on to long, thin metal skewers, 1" apart.
- Grill the kebabs under a medium-hot gas or electric grill as described on pp. xiv–xv for 6–8 minutes.
- Baste with oil, turn the skewers and grill again for another 5–6 minutes.
- Slip the kebabs off the skewers on to a serving platter and serve hot with garlic flatbread (p. 31).

LEBANESE CHICKEN KEBABS
SHISH TOUK
Makes 2–3

Shish is the Turkish word for skewer, though is also the Farsi word for six. Shish kebab is a dish comprising meat threaded on a skewer and grilled. Any kind of meat may be used and cubes of fruits or vegetables are often threaded on the skewers as well. Normally, vegetables include aubergine, bell pepper, mushroom, onion and tomato.

Chicken breast, boneless, without skin 500 gm
Olive oil, for basting 2 tbsp

Marinade
Garlic paste 1 tbsp
Olive oil 2 tbsp
Lime juice 3 tbsp
Cumin powder 1 tsp
Garam masala powder or allspice powder ½ tsp
Cinnamon powder ¼ tsp
Black pepper, freshly ground ½ tsp
Salt 1 tsp

• Wash the chicken and pat dry with paper towels. Cut it into 1" cubes.

Marination
• Combine the ingredients for the marinade in a bowl and whisk, till they blend well.
• Add the chicken and mix well, to ensure that it is completely coated with the marinade.
• Cover and set aside to marinate in the refrigerator for 4–5 hours.

For the kebabs
- Remove the chicken from the refrigerator 30 minutes before cooking it.
- Thread the chicken on to long, thin metal skewers, 1" apart.
- Grill the kebabs over a charcoal fire; or under a very hot gas or electric grill as described on pp. xiv–xv for 6–7 minutes.
- Baste with olive oil, turn the skewers and grill again for another 3–4 minutes, till delicately browned.
- Slip the kebabs off the skewers on to a serving platter.
- Serve hot with baked pita bread (p. 24), hummus and a green salad with feta cheese (see p. 21).

CHICKEN RUM KEBABS

Makes 4–6

We have all marinated chicken with wine, but this time I tried it with rum and the result was outstanding. I hope you enjoy this dish as much as I did.

Chicken breast, boneless, without skin 1 kg
Oil, for basting 3 tbsp
Oregano, fresh, chopped ½ tsp

First marinade
Ginger paste 2 tbsp
Garlic paste 2 tbsp
Lime juice 1 tbsp
White vinegar 1 tsp
Sugar ¼ tsp
Salt 2½ tsp

Second marinade
Rum ½ cup
Soy sauce ¼ cup
Orange juice ¼ cup
Mustard powder 1 tsp
Black pepper, freshly ground 1 tsp
Red chilli powder 1 tsp
Coriander powder ½ tsp
Cinnamon powder ¼ tsp
Sugar, powdered ¼ tsp

- Wash the chicken and pat dry with paper towels. Cut it into 1" cubes.

First marination
- Combine the ingredients for the first marinade in a bowl and whisk, till they blend well.

- Add the chicken and mix well, to ensure that it is completely coated with the marinade.
- Cover and set aside to marinate in the refrigerator for about 30 minutes.

Second marination
- Combine the ingredients for the second marinade in another bowl and whisk, till they blend well.
- Add the marinated chicken and mix well, to ensure that it is completely coated with the second marinade.
- Cover and set aside to marinate in the refrigerator overnight.

For the kebabs
- Remove the chicken from the refrigerator and bring to room temperature.
- Thread the chicken on to long, thin metal skewers, 1" apart.
- Grill the kebabs under a very hot gas or electric grill as described on pp. xiv–xv for 7–8 minutes.
- Baste with oil, turn the skewers and grill again for another 3–4 minutes or till the chicken is tender.
- Slip the kebabs off the skewers on to a serving platter. Sprinkle oregano on top and serve with chilli garlic chutney (p. 11) and Turkish lavash (p. 29).

IRANIAN CHICKEN KEBABS

JOOJEH KEBAB

Makes 4

Another favourite Iranian kebab. It has a unique marinade and it is recommended that you use boneless chicken breast.

Chicken breast, boneless, without skin 450 gm
Parsley, fresh, chopped 1 tsp

Marinade
Olive oil ½ cup
Lime juice 1 tbsp
White onion, large, grated 1
Saffron strands about 10
Red chilli powder ½ tsp
Cumin powder 1 tsp (optional)
Salt 1 tsp
Black pepper, freshly ground 1 tsp

- Rinse the chicken with cold water and pat dry with paper towels. Cut into 1" chunks.

Marination
- Put the ingredients for the marinade in a bowl. Add 1 tbsp of water and whisk, till well blended.
- Add the chicken and mix well, to ensure that it is completely coated with the marinade.
- Cover and set aside to marinate overnight in the refrigerator.

For the kebabs
- Remove the chicken from the refrigerator and bring to room temperature.
- Thread the chicken on to long, thin metal skewers, 1" apart.
- Grill the kebabs over a charcoal fire or under a medium-hot

gas or electric grill as described on pp. xiv–xv for 15–20 minutes, turning periodically and basting with leftover marinade.
- Serve the joojeh kebabs sprinkled with parsley over a bed of steamed basmati rice or grilled vegetables and Irani raita (p. 19).

HONEY CHICKEN KEBABS

Makes 3–4

This is a simple recipe in which honey, cinnamon and nutmeg lend a delicious flavour and aroma to the chicken. I hope you enjoy one of my special recipes.

Chicken, boneless, without skin 800 gm
Garlic, chopped 2 cloves
Onions, small, cut into 1½" pieces 5
Red bell peppers, cut into 1½" pieces 2
Parsley, fresh, chopped 1 tsp

Marinade
Oil ¼ cup
Honey ⅓ cup
Soy sauce ⅓ cup
Red chilli powder ½
Cumin powder ½ tsp
Cinnamon powder 1¼ tsp
Green cardamom powder ½ tsp
Nutmeg powder ¼ tsp
Black pepper, freshly ground ½ tsp
Salt 2 tsp

- Wash the chicken and pat dry with paper towels. Cut it into 1" cubes.

Marination
- Combine the ingredients for the marinade in a bowl and whisk, till they blend well.
- Remove 1–2 tbsp and set aside for basting.
- Add the chicken, garlic, onions and peppers to the bowl and mix well, to ensure they are completely coated with the marinade.

- Set aside to marinate in the refrigerator for at least 4–5 hours or overnight.

For the kebabs
- Remove the chicken from the refrigerator and bring to room temperature.
- Drain the marinade from the chicken and vegetables.
- Thread the chicken and vegetables alternately on to long, thin metal skewers, 1" apart.
- Grill the kebabs under a very hot gas or electric grill as described on pp. xiv–xv for 12–15 minutes.
- Baste with the reserved marinade, turn the skewers and grill again for another 5–6 minutes.
- Slip the kebabs off the skewers on to a serving platter and sprinkle parsley on top.
- Serve hot with mint chutney (p. 12).

MOROCCAN CHICKEN KEBABS

Makes 3–4

A simple and delicious Moroccan delicacy. I learnt it from a Moroccan chef during my visit to the Kulinart show in Frankfurt. Try the kebab with the Moroccan flatbread.

Chicken breast 750 gm
Oil, for basting 3 tbsp
Parsley, fresh, chopped 1 tsp

Marinade
Parsley, fresh, chopped 2 tbsp
Ginger paste ½ tsp
Garlic, chopped fine 2 cloves
Lime juice 2 tbsp
Olive oil 2 tbsp
Turmeric powder ½ tsp
Red chilli powder 2 tsp
Coriander powder ½ tsp
White pepper powder ½ tsp
Saffron strands, crushed ½ tsp
Salt 1½ tsp
Sea salt ½ tsp

- Wash the chicken and pat dry with paper towels. Cut it into ¾" cubes.

Marination
- Combine the ingredients for the marinade in a bowl and whisk, till they blend well.
- Add the chicken and mix well, to ensure that it is completely coated with the marinade.
- Cover and set aside to marinate in the refrigerator for several hours or overnight.

For the kebabs

- Remove the chicken from the refrigerator and bring to room temperature.
- Thread the chicken on to long, thin metal skewers, 1" apart.
- Grill the kebabs under a very hot gas or electric grill as described on pp. xiv–xv for 6–7 minutes.
- Baste with oil, turn the skewers and grill again for another 3–4 minutes.
- Slip the kebabs off the skewers on to a serving platter and sprinkle parsley on top.
- Serve immediately with Moroccan flatbread (p. 30) and a garlic dip.

NOTE:

This dish can be prepared with turkey as well.

PESTO CHICKEN KEBABS

Makes 3–4

I have great memories of this dish. On one of my recent trips to Rome on a family holiday, our Italian friend invited us to her home for a barbeque and served this delicious chicken dish with raisin salad, a delectable cheese, and aubergine sautéed in butter and garlic. We ended with tiramisu.

Chicken breast, boneless, without skin 600 gm
Lime juice 2 tsp
Olive oil 2 tsp
Sour cream 2 tbsp

First marinade
Ginger paste 1 tsp
Garlic, minced 2 tsp
Coriander powder 1 tsp
Lime juice 2 tsp
Salt 1 tsp

Second marinade
Yogurt, hung, whisked 2 tbsp (p. 5)
Pesto sauce, commercial 1 tbsp
Refined oil 3 tbsp
Black pepper, freshly ground ½ tsp

- Wash the chicken and pat dry with paper towels. Cut it into 1" cubes.

First marination
- Combine the ingredients for the first marinade in a bowl and whisk, till they blend well.
- Add the chicken and rub in the marinade so that it is completely coated.

- Cover and set aside to marinate in the refrigerator for about 1 hour.

Second marination
- Combine the ingredients for the second marinade in another bowl and whisk, till they blend well.
- Add the marinated chicken and mix well, to ensure that it is completely coated with the second marinade.
- Cover and set aside to marinate in the refrigerator for 2–4 hours.

For the kebabs
- Remove the chicken from the refrigerator and bring to room temperature.
- Thread the chicken on to long, thin metal skewers, 1" apart.
- Grill the kebabs under a very hot gas or electric grill as described on pp. xiv–xv for 5–7 minutes.
- Baste with olive oil and lime juice, turn the skewers and grill again for another 5–6 minutes.
- Slip the kebabs off the skewers on to a serving platter and serve hot with sour cream and Italian flatbread (p. 26).

PISTACHIO CHICKEN KEBABS

Makes 2–3

It's a joke in my family that I can eat anything green. I love pistachio and almost everything made with it, such as pistachio burfi (an Indian dessert), ice cream, muffins . . . And the same goes for pistachio chicken kebabs, one of my creations.

Chicken, boneless, without skin 500 gm
Ghee, melted, for basting 2 tbsp

First marinade
Ginger paste 1 tsp
Garlic paste 1 tsp
Lime juice 1 tsp
White vinegar ½ tsp
Coriander powder 1 tsp
Salt 2 tsp

Second marinade
Yogurt, hung, whisked 8 tbsp (p. 5)
Lime juice 2 tbsp
Cream, fresh, whisked 1 tbsp
Refined oil 2 tbsp
Pistachio flakes 2 tsp
Yellow chilli powder ½ tsp
Salt 2 tsp

Pistachio paste
Pistachios 3 tbsp
Green chillies, seeded 2
Curry leaves, fresh 10
Coriander leaves, fresh 1 cup
Puréed spinach 1 tbsp

- Wash the chicken and pat dry with paper towels. Cut it into 6 pieces.

First marination
- Combine the ingredients for the first marinade in a bowl and whisk, till they blend well.
- Add the chicken and mix well, to ensure that it is completely coated with the marinade.
- Cover and set aside to marinate in the refrigerator for about 30 minutes.

Second marination
- Combine the ingredients for the second marinade in another bowl and whisk, till they blend well.
- Add the marinated chicken and mix well, to ensure that it is completely coated with the second marinade.
- Cover and set aside to marinate in the refrigerator for 5–6 hours.

Pistachio paste
- Grind the ingredients for the pistachio paste to a smooth consistency.
- Dip the marinated chicken in the paste and rub well.
- Set aside in the refrigerator for 7–8 hours

For the kebabs
- Remove the chicken from the refrigerator and bring to room temperature.
- Thread the chicken on to long, thin metal skewers, 1" apart.
- Grill the kebabs under a very hot gas or electric grill as described on pp. xiv–xv for 7–8 minutes.
- Baste with melted ghee, turn the skewers and grill again for another 3–4 minutes or till the chicken is tender.
- Slip the kebabs off the skewers on to a serving platter.
- Serve hot with mint chutney (p. 12) and a salad.

TERIYAKI CHICKEN KEBABS

Makes 2–3

When I created this dish, I was inspired by the lightness of Japanese cuisine and the awesome teriyaki sauce. I guess you will love this dish as much as my son Gunav does.

Chicken breast, boneless, without skin 800 gm
Red bell pepper 1
Yellow bell pepper 1
White onion, large 1
Mushrooms, kept whole 1½ cups
Oil, for basting 4 tbsp
Coriander leaves, fresh, chopped 1/3 cup
Sesame seeds, white, roasted 1 tsp

Marinade
Teriyaki sauce ½ cup (p. 17)
Honey 1/3 cup
Dry sherry ¼ cup
Ginger paste ½ tsp
Garlic powder 1½ tsp
Red chilli powder 2 tsp
Coriander powder 1 tsp
Nutmeg, freshly grated ½ tsp
Sugar ½ tsp
Salt 2 tsp

- Wash the chicken and pat dry with paper towels. Cut into 1" cubes.
- Cut the bell pepper into 2" pieces.
- Cut the onion into quarters and separate the layers.
- Leave the mushrooms whole.

Marination
- Combine the ingredients for the marinade in a bowl and whisk, till they blend well.
- Add the chicken and vegetables and mix well, to ensure that they are completely coated with the marinade.
- Cover and set aside to marinate in the refrigerator overnight.

For the kebabs
- Remove the chicken from the refrigerator and bring to room temperature.
- Thread the chicken and vegetables alternately on to long, thin metal skewers, 1" apart.
- Grill the kebabs under a very hot gas or electric grill as described on pp. xiv–xv for 7–8 minutes.
- Baste with oil, turn the skewers and grill again for another 6–7 minutes, till the meat and vegetables are tender.
- Slip the chicken and vegetables off the skewers on to a serving platter. Sprinkle coriander leaves and sesame seeds on top and serve hot.

NOTE:
- This dish can be made with beef sirloin as well.
- Vegetarians can make a delicious version using a variety of vegetables—zucchini wedges, portabella mushrooms, water chestnuts, cherry tomatoes, pineapple chunks, marinated with teriyaki sauce and grilled to perfection.

GREEK CHICKEN KEBABS WITH FETA MINT SAUCE

Makes 2–3

These are kebabs from the beautiful Greek islands. The feta mint sauce makes these kebabs quite unique. Enjoy them with crisp naan or pita bread.

Chicken thighs, boneless, without skin 750 gm
Zucchini 1
Red onion, small ½
Olive oil 2 tbsp
Parsley, fresh, chopped 1 tsp
Lime, cut into wedges 1

Marinade
Olive oil 2 tbsp
Red wine vinegar 2 tbsp
Oregano, dried ½ tsp
Black pepper, freshly ground 1 tsp
Salt 1 tsp
Sea salt 1½ tsp

Feta mint sauce
Feta cheese, crumbled ½ cup
Yogurt ½ cup
Red wine vinegar 1½ tbsp
Mint leaves, fresh, chopped 1 cup
Cumin seeds, roasted 1 tsp
White pepper, freshly ground 1 tsp

- Wash the chicken and pat dry with paper towels. Cut it into 16 cubes of 2" each.
- Cut the zucchini in half lengthwise and cut crosswise into 16 pieces, 1" each.

- Peel the onion, cut into quarters and separate the layers.

Marination
- Combine the ingredients for the marinade in a bowl and whisk, till they blend well.
- Add the chicken, zucchini and onion and mix well, to ensure that they are completely coated with the marinade.
- Cover and set aside to marinate in the refrigerator overnight.

Feta mint sauce
- Blend the ingredients for the sauce, till smooth.
- Refrigerate till required.

For the kebabs
- Remove the chicken from the refrigerator and bring to room temperature.
- Thread 3 pieces of chicken and 2 each of the zucchini and onion alternately on long, thin metal skewers, 1" apart.
- Grill the kebabs under a very hot gas or electric grill as described on pp. xiv–xv for 7–8 minutes.
- Baste with olive oil, turn the skewers and grill again for another 4–5 minutes.
- Slip the kebabs off the skewers on to a serving platter. Sprinkle parsley on top and serve hot with mint feta sauce, lime wedges and crisp naan (p. 33) or pita bread (p. 24).

RED CURRY CHICKEN KEBABS

Makes 2–3

I love my Thai curries and here is an attempt to use the Thai curry with kebab.

Chicken breast, boneless, without skin 700 gm
Red bell pepper 1
Zucchini 1
Onion 1
Parsley, fresh, chopped 1 tsp
Lime cut into wedges 1

Marinade
Coconut milk 2 tbsp
Thai red curry paste 2 tbsp
Lemon grass, chopped fine 1 stalk
Sugar ½ tsp
Salt 2 tsp

- Wash the chicken and pat dry with paper towels. Cut it into large chunks.
- Cut the zucchini in half lengthwise and cut crosswise into large chunks, the same size as the chicken.
- Peel the onion, cut into quarters and separate the layers.

Marination
- Pour the coconut milk and red curry paste into a bowl. Whisk till well blended.
- Add the remaining ingredients for the marinade and mix again.
- Add the chicken and vegetables and mix well to ensure that they are completely coated with the marinade.
- Cover and set aside to marinate in the refrigerator for 3–4 hours.

For the kebabs
- Remove the chicken and vegetables from the refrigerator and bring to room temperature.
- Thread the chicken and vegetables alternately on to long, thin metal skewers, 1" apart.
- Grill the kebabs under a very hot gas or electric grill as described on pp. xiv–xv for 7–8 minutes.
- Baste with the leftover marinade, turn the skewers and grill again for another 4–5 minutes.
- Slip the chicken and vegetables off the skewers on to a serving platter. Sprinkle parsley on top and serve hot with lime wedges.

GRILLED CHICKEN, RED ONION AND MINT KEBABS WITH GREEK SALAD

Makes 2–3

When you are in the mood to have a healthy meal do choose these mint-flavoured kebabs. As a true Punjabi my food is incomplete without onion and pudina (mint) chutney. So I thought why not make a meal with both of my favourite ingredients.

Chicken breast, boneless, without skin 750 gm
Red onions 2
Salt 1 tsp
Black pepper, freshly ground 1 tsp
Parsley, fresh, chopped 1 tsp

Marinade
Olive oil 2 tbsp
Ginger paste 1 tsp
Garlic paste 1 tbsp
Mint leaves, fresh ½ cup
Mint leaves, dried 1 tsp
Oregano, dried 1 tsp
Red chilli powder 1 tsp
Cumin powder ½ tsp
Black pepper, freshly ground 1 tsp
Salt 1 tsp

Basting sauce
Olive oil 2 tbsp
Lime juice 2 tbsp

- Wash the chicken and pat dry with paper towels. Cut it into 1″ cubes.
- Cut the onions into quarters and separate the layers.

Marination

- Combine the ingredients for the marinade in a bowl and whisk, till they blend well.
- Add the chicken and onions and mix well, to ensure that they are completely coated with the marinade.
- Cover and set aside to marinate in the refrigerator for 4–5 hours.

For the kebabs

- Remove the chicken from the refrigerator and bring to room temperature.
- Whisk the ingredients for the basting sauce in a small bowl.
- Thread the chicken and onions alternately on to long, thin metal skewers, 1" apart.
- Sprinkle with salt and pepper.
- Grill the kebabs under a very hot gas or electric grill as described on pp. xiv–xv for 7–8 minutes.
- Brush with the basting sauce, turn the skewers and grill again for another 5–6 minutes.
- Slip the kebabs off the skewers on to a serving platter and sprinkle parsley on top.
- Serve hot with garlic flatbread (p. 31) and Greek salad (p. 21) on the side.

ALMOND CHICKEN

MURGH BADAM PASANDA

Makes 4

A chicken kebab cooked with almonds and yogurt, this is popular in India and Pakistan. And as the name *pasanda* suggests, it is a favoured dish for most people.

Chicken breasts 8
Ghee, for basting 2 tbsp

Marinade
Ginger paste 5 tsp
Yogurt, hung, whisked 1¼ cups (p. 5)
Garlic paste 5 tsp
Cumin powder 1 tsp
Salt 2 tsp

Garnish
Almonds 2 tbsp
Ghee 1 tbsp
Coriander leaves, fresh, chopped 5 tbsp

Gravy
Ghee 2 tbsp
Green cardamoms 5
Cloves 8
Onion, medium-sized, sliced 1
Tomatoes, medium-sized, chopped 3
Red chilli powder 2½ tsp
Black pepper powder 1 tsp
Refined flour/maida 5 tsp
Chicken stock 500 ml
Nutmeg powder 1 tsp
Mace powder 1 tsp

Saffron strands ½ tsp, dissolved in 2 tbsp of milk
Almond essence 1 tsp
Salt 1½ tsp

- Wash the chicken and drain thoroughly.
- Put the pieces between wet cling-film sheets and flatten them lightly with a mallet or rolling pin into 3"-long pasanda.
- Pat dry with paper towels.

Marination
- Rub the ginger paste over the chicken pieces.
- Whisk the yogurt in a large bowl with the garlic paste and salt.
- Add the chicken and rub in the marinade so that it is completely coated.
- Cover and set aside to marinate in the refrigerator for about 1 hour.

Garnish
- Soak the almonds in boiling water for 10 minutes. Drain and peel.
- Sliver the almonds and fry them in the ghee on medium heat, till golden.
- Drain on kitchen paper and set aside.

Chicken
- Remove the chicken from the refrigerator and bring to room temperature.
- Heat the ghee on a tava or griddle and fry the chicken pieces on medium heat, turning them periodically, till half cooked.
- Drain on kitchen paper.

Gravy
- Heat the ghee in a pan and sauté the cardamoms and cloves on medium heat, till they splutter.
- Add the onions and sauté, till golden brown.

- Stir in the tomatoes, chilli powder, pepper and flour and stir for a few minutes.
- Pour in the stock and stir vigorously to avoid lumps.
- Simmer on medium to high heat, till the gravy is thick.
- Immerse the chicken in the thick gravy.
- Cook on medium heat, stirring frequently for about 10 minutes, till the chicken is tender.
- Add the nutmeg powder, mace powder, saffron milk and almond essence and stir for 1 minute.
- Spoon the chicken into a serving platter, garnish with fried almonds and coriander leaves and serve hot.

AFGHANI CHICKEN

Makes 4

On the kebab trail, this one is a milestone and popular on the Moti Mahal menu. Chicken on the bone, marinated with fresh cream and cashew nut, this tender, succulent kebab is a Punjabi delight!

Chicken, kept whole 600 gm
Butter, melted, for basting 3 tbsp

First marinade
Ginger-garlic paste ½ tbsp
Lime juice 2 tbsp
Salt 2 tsp

Second marinade
Cashew nut and cheese paste ½ cup (p. 6)
Cream, fresh, whisked 5 tsp
Egg, whisked 1
White pepper, freshly ground 1 tsp
Green cardamom powder 1 tsp

- Wash the chicken and pat dry with paper towels. Cut it into 8 pieces.

First marination
- Combine the ingredients for the first marinade in a bowl and whisk, till they blend well.
- Add the chicken and rub in the marinade so that it is completely coated.
- Cover and set aside to marinate in the refrigerator for about 1 hour.

Second marination

- Combine the ingredients for the second marinade in a bowl and whisk, till they blend well.
- Add the marinated chicken and mix well, to ensure that it is completely coated with the second marinade.
- Cover and set aside to marinate in the refrigerator for 3–4 hours.

For the kebabs

- Remove the chicken from the refrigerator and bring to room temperature.
- Thread the chicken on to long, thin metal skewers, 1" apart.
- Cook the kebabs in a medium-hot tandoor or grill over a charcoal fire as described on pp. xiv–xv for 6–7 minutes.
- Baste with melted butter, turn the skewers and grill again for another 3–4 minutes.
- Slip the kebabs off the skewers on to a serving platter and serve hot with mint chutney (p. 12). I love it with makhan roti (p. 34).

STUFFED CHICKEN DRUMSTICKS

BHARWAN TANGRI KEBAB

Makes 8

Yet another favourite on the Moti Mahal menu. Tender drumsticks with a stuffing of minced chicken and cashew nuts is a popular starter.

Chicken drumsticks 16
Butter, melted, for basting 4 tbsp

Stuffing
Oil 3 tbsp
Cashew nuts, ground ¾ tsp
Chicken, boneless, without skin, minced 300 gm
Coriander leaves, fresh, chopped 5 tbsp
Saffron strands a pinch
Garam masala powder 1 tsp
Green cardamom powder ½ tsp
Salt 1½ tsp

First marinade
Ginger-garlic paste 1 tsp
Lime juice 2 tsp
White pepper powder 1 tsp
Salt 1 tsp

Second marinade
Processed Cheddar cheese, grated 200 gm
Egg white, whisked 1
Cream, fresh, whisked 1¾ cups
Ginger-garlic paste 1 tsp
Coriander leaves, fresh, chopped 1 tbsp
Cumin powder 1/3 tsp
Green cardamom powder ¼ tsp
Mace powder ¼ tsp

- Wash the chicken drumsticks and pat dry with paper towels.
- Slit the chicken flesh along the bone with a sharp knife.
- Make 2 incisions on the back of the drumsticks.

Stuffing
- Heat the oil in a pan. Add cashew nuts and chicken mince and sauté on medium heat, till the meat turns white.
- Add the remaining ingredients for the stuffing and continue to sauté, till the mix becomes completely dry.
- Remove from heat and set aside to cool.
- Divide the kebab mix into 16 equal portions and stuff the drumsticks and the incisions. Press the chicken flesh carefully over the stuffing.

First marination
- Combine the ingredients for the first marinade in a bowl and whisk, till they blend well.
- Add the drumsticks and mix gently, to ensure that they are completely coated with the marinade. Be careful that the stuffing does not fall out.
- Cover and set aside to marinate in the refrigerator for about 1 hour.

Second marination
- Put the cheese and egg white in a deep tray and mix with your hands, till they blend.
- Pour in the cream and continue to mix, till smooth.
- Add the remaining ingredients for the second marinade and whisk, till they blend well.
- Add the marinated drumsticks and mix gently, to ensure that they are completely coated with the second marinade. Be careful that the stuffing does not fall out.
- Cover and set aside to marinate in the refrigerator for at least 2 hours.

For the kebabs
- Remove the drumsticks from the refrigerator and bring to room temperature.
- Thread the drumsticks on to long, thin metal skewers, 1" apart.
- Cook the kebabs in a medium-hot tandoor or grill under a very hot gas or electric grill as described on pp. xiv–xv for 9–10 minutes.
- Baste with melted butter, turn the skewers and grill again for another 3–4 minutes.
- Slip the drumsticks off the skewers on to a serving platter and serve hot with mint chutney (p. 12).

TANDOORI CHICKEN

Makes 2–4

In the introduction I've told you the story of how my grandfather invented the tandoori chicken. Here is the famous recipe.

Chicken, kept whole 1 (750 gm)
Chaat masala powder 1 tsp
Onion, sliced in rings 1
Lime, cut in wedges 1

First marinade
Lime juice 1½ tbsp
Red chilli powder ½ tsp
Salt 1 tsp

Second marinade
Yogurt, hung, whisked ½ cup (p. 5)
Ginger paste 1 tbsp
Garlic paste 1 tbsp
Fenugreek leaves, dried, powdered ½ tsp
Garam masala powder 1 tsp
Rock salt ½ tsp
Salt 1 tsp

- Clean the chicken, remove the skin, backbone and wing tips. Wash and pat dry with paper towels. Cut it into 4 pieces.
- Make deep incisions on the breast, thighs and drumsticks.

First marination
- Combine the ingredients for the first marinade in a bowl and whisk, till they blend well.
- Add the chicken and mix well, to ensure that it is completely coated with the marinade.

- Cover and set aside in the refrigerator to marinate for about 30 minutes, turning the pieces occasionally.

Second marination
- Combine the ingredients for the second marinade in another bowl and whisk, till they blend well.
- Add the marinated chicken and mix well, to ensure that it is completely coated with the second marinade.
- Cover and set aside in the refrigerator to marinate for another 8–10 hours, turning the pieces occasionally.

For the chicken
- Remove the chicken from the refrigerator and bring to room temperature.
- Thread the chicken on to long, thin metal skewers, 1" apart.
- Cook the chicken in a hot tandoor or grill under a hot gas or electric grill as described on pp. xiv–xv for about 5–6 minutes.
- Baste with the leftover marinade, turn the skewers and grill again for another 6–7 minutes, till the juices run clear when the flesh is pierced with a fork.
- Slip the chicken off the skewers on to a serving platter. Sprinkle chaat masala powder and onion rings on top and serve immediately with lime wedges and mint chutney (p. 12) on the side.

TANDOORI DUCK

Makes 8

We are born in the land of tandoori chicken, so where does the duck fit in? I thought why not experiment with another bird. Duck meat is a little hard, so remember to marinate it at least overnight and in some cases try using a tenderizer. I suggest you have it with plum sauce and pita bread.

Duck, kept whole 1 (2 kg)
Sumac 2 tsp
Coriander leaves, fresh, chopped 1 tbsp

Marinade
Yogurt, hung, whisked 1 cup (p. 5)
Ginger minced 1 tbsp
Garlic, crushed 3 cloves
White vinegar 1 tbsp
Oil 2 tbsp
Red chilli powder 1 tsp
Cumin powder 1 tbsp
Black pepper powder 1 tbsp
Sea salt 1½ tsp

- Clean the duck, remove the skin, backbone and wing tips. Wash and pat dry with paper towels. Cut it into 4 pieces.
- Make deep incisions on the breast, thighs and drumsticks with a sharp knife.

Marination
- Combine the ingredients for the marinade in a bowl and whisk, till they blend well.
- Add the duck and mix well, to ensure that it is completely coated with the marinade.
- Cover and set aside in the refrigerator to marinate for about 24 hours, turning the pieces occasionally.

For the duck

- Remove the duck from the refrigerator and bring to room temperature.
- Thread the pieces on to long, thin metal skewers, 1" apart.
- Cook the duck in a hot tandoor or grill under a hot gas or electric grill as described on pp. xiv–xv for 5–6 minutes.
- Baste with the leftover marinade, turn the skewers and grill again for another 6–7 minutes, till the juices run clear when the flesh is pierced with a fork.
- Slip the duck pieces off the skewers on to a serving platter. Sprinkle sumac and coriander leaves on top and serve immediately with any salad of your choice.

TANDOORI QUAIL

Makes 2

This was relished by older generations, but today's youngsters know little about such delicacies as quail.

Quails, farmed, without skin, kept whole 2 (125 gm each)
Oil, for basting 2 tbsp

First marinade
Ginger paste 1 tsp
Garlic paste 1 tsp
Lime juice 2 tbsp
Salt 2 tsp
Rock salt 1 tsp

Second marinade
Yogurt, hung, whisked 4 tbsp (p. 5)
Cashew nut paste 4 tsp (p. 90)
Cream, fresh, whisked ¼ cup
Green chillies, seeded, chopped fine 2
Coriander leaves, fresh, chopped fine 1 tsp
Ginger paste ½ tsp
Garlic paste 1 tsp
Water melon seeds, ground to a paste 2 tsp
Black pepper powder 1 tsp
Garam masala powder 1 tsp
Green cardamom powder 1 tsp

· Clean and wash the quails. Pat dry with paper towels. Make 2 deep insertions with a sharp knife on the breasts and each leg.

First marination
· Combine the ingredients for the first marinade in a bowl and whisk, till they blend well.

- Add the quails and mix well, to ensure that they are completely coated with the marinade.
- Cover and set aside to marinate in the refrigerator for about 30 minutes.

Second marination
- Whisk the yogurt in a deep bowl. Add the remaining ingredients for the second marinade and whisk, till they blend well.
- Add the marinated quails and mix well, to ensure that they are completely coated with the second marinade.
- Cover and set aside to marinate in the refrigerator for 7–8 hours.

For the quails
- Remove the quails from the refrigerator and bring to room temperature.
- Thread each quail on a long, thin metal skewer.
- Cook the quails in a medium-hot tandoor or grill under a very hot gas or electric grill as described on pp. xiv–xv for 7–8 minutes.
- Baste with oil, turn the skewers and cook again for another 3–4 minutes, till the juices run clear when the flesh is pierced with a fork.
- Slip the quails off the skewers on to a serving platter.
- Serve hot with mint chutney (p. 12).

SEAFOOD

AMRITSARI FISH

Makes 2

A favourite fish recipe from Punjab, this is the Indian version of Britain's fish and chips.

It is served in almost every restaurant in Punjab, and is a must on most non-vegetarian wedding menus.

Pomfret, boneless 250 gm
Oil for frying

First marinade
Ginger paste 1 tsp
Garlic paste 1 tsp
Lime juice 1 tbsp
Red chilli powder 1 tsp

Second marinade
Egg, whisked 1
Ginger paste ½ tsp
Garlic paste 1 tsp
Carom seeds ½ tsp
Gram flour 100 gm
Cornflour 1 tsp
Lime juice 1 tsp
Red chilli paste 1 tsp
Coriander powder ½ tsp
Salt 1½ tsp

- Wash the fish and pat dry with paper towels. Cut it into 2" fillets.

First marination

- Combine the ingredients for the first marinade in a bowl and whisk till they blend well.
- Add the fish and mix well, to ensure that it is completely coated with the marinade
- Cover and set aside to marinate in the refrigerator for 30 minutes.

Second marination

- Combine the ingredients for the second marinade in another bowl and whisk till they blend well.
- Add the marinated fish and mix well, to ensure that it is completely coated with the second marinade.
- Cover and set aside to marinate in the refrigerator for 2–3 hours.

For the fish

- Remove the fish from the refrigerator and bring to room temperature.
- Heat the oil in a frying pan. Add the fish and fry on medium heat, on both sides, till golden brown and cooked through.
- Drain on kitchen paper.
- Serve hot with a salad and mint chutney (p. 12). I tried it with Turkish lavash (p. 29) and it was divine!

TANDOORI POMFRET

Makes 4–6

This dish appeared on the very first menu of Moti Mahal and remains there to this day. One of my grandfather's favourites, he would order it nearly every day.

Pomfret, kept whole 4 (about 350 gm each)
Butter, melted, for basting 4 tbsp

First marinade
Ginger paste 4 tsp
Garlic paste 4 tsp
Red chilli powder ½ tsp
Lime juice 4 tbsp
Carom seeds 1 tbsp
Salt 4 tsp

Second marinade
Yogurt, hung, whisked 2 cups (p. 5)
Gram flour, roasted 2 tbsp
Oil ¼ cup
Turmeric powder ½ tsp
Cumin powder 1 tsp
Garam masala powder 1 tbsp

- Clean the fish, trim the tails and fins and wash thoroughly. Pat dry with paper towels.
- Make 3–4 incisions with a sharp knife across both sides of each fish.

First marination
- Combine the ingredients for the first marinade in a bowl and whisk well.
- Add the fish and rub in the marinade on both sides, to ensure that they are completely coated with the marinade.

- Cover and set aside to marinate in the refrigerator for 30 minutes.

Second marination
- Whisk the yogurt with the remaining ingredients for the second marinade in another bowl.
- Drain the marinated fish and add them to the pan.
- Rub the fish with the marinade, to coat completely.
- Cover and set aside to marinate in the refrigerator for 3–4 hours.

For the fish
- Remove the fish from the refrigerator and bring to room temperature.
- Thread each fish horizontally on to a long, thin metal skewer.
- Cook the fish in a medium-hot tandoor; or grill under a hot gas or electric grill as described on pp. xiv–xv for 8–10 minutes.
- Baste with melted butter, turn the skewers and grill again for another 3–4 minutes.
- Slip the fish off the skewers on to a serving platter.
- Serve hot with a salad and mint chutney (p. 12).

TANDOORI SALMON

Makes 4–6

This is a delicacy the world over for people who savour pink salmon—grilled, sautéed or in a nice salad. However, I choose to make it in a tandoor and the result is phenomenal.

Salmon, boneless 1 kg
Olive oil, for basting 3 tbsp

First marinade
Garlic paste 1 tsp
Lime juice 3 tbsp
Black pepper powder 2 tsp
Salt 3 tsp

Second marinade
Yogurt, hung, whisked 1 cup (p. 5)
Olive oil 4 tsp
Green chilli, seeded, chopped 5
Garlic paste 4 tsp
Coriander leaves, fresh, chopped 1 tsp
Dill leaves, fresh, chopped 2 tsp

- Wash the fish and pat dry with paper towels. Cut it into 1½" cubes.

First marination
- Combine the ingredients for the first marinade in a bowl and whisk till they blend well.
- Add the fish and mix well, to ensure that it is completely coated with the marinade.
- Cover and set aside to marinate in the refrigerator for 30 minutes.

Second marination

- Whisk the yogurt with the remaining ingredients for the second marinade in another bowl, till they blend well.
- Drain the marinated fish and add it to the bowl.
- Mix well, to ensure that it is completely coated with the second marinade.
- Cover and set aside to marinate in the refrigerator for 3–4 hours.

For the fish

- Remove the fish from the refrigerator and bring to room temperature.
- Thread the fish on to long, thin metal skewers, 1" apart.
- Cook the fish in a medium-hot tandoor; or grill under a hot gas or electric grill as described on pp. xiv–xv for about 10 minutes.
- Baste with olive oil, turn the skewers and grill again for another 3–4 minutes.
- Slip the kebabs off the skewers on to a serving platter.
- Serve hot with onion rings.

FISH KEBABS

MACHCHI TIKKA

Makes 2–3

The British foreign secretary, Sir Robin Cook, while addressing a think tank in London in April 2001, claimed that chicken tikka masala was one of Britain's true national dishes. This led to great speculation regarding the origin of this popular and delicious dish. The majority of votes indicated that it is a derivative of the butter chicken, introduced by Moti Mahal's Kundan Lal Gujral almost 60 years ago.

I took the liberty of reinventing the dish by substituting chicken with fish and the result was phenomenal, as you will see after trying my recipe.

Sole fish, boneless 500 gm
Lime juice 1 tbsp
Oil, for basting 2 tbsp
Chaat masala powder 1 tbsp

First marinade
Lime juice 2 tbsp
Red chilli powder 1 tsp
Salt 1 tsp

Second marinade
Yogurt, hung, whisked 3 tbsp (p. 5)
Ginger paste 1 tsp
Garlic paste 2 tsp
Carom seeds ½ tsp
Gram flour 2 tbsp
Fenugreek seeds 1 tsp
Red tandoori food colour 2 drops (optional)
Salt 1½ tsp

- Wash the fish and pat dry with paper towels. Cut it into 2"
  cubes.
- Rub with 1 tbsp of lime juice, rinse and pat dry again.

First marination
- Combine the ingredients for the first marinade in a bowl and
  whisk, till they blend well.
- Add the fish and mix well, to ensure that it is completely
  coated with the marinade.
- Cover and set aside to marinate in the refrigerator for 30
  minutes.

Second marination
- Combine the ingredients for the second marinade, except the
  gram flour, in another bowl and whisk, till well blended.
- Add the marinated fish and mix well, to ensure that it is
  completely coated with the second marinade.
- Sprinkle in the gram flour and mix again.
- Cover and set aside to marinate in the refrigerator for 30
  minutes.

For the tikkas
- Remove the fish from the refrigerator and bring to room
  temperature.
- Thread the fish on to long, thin metal skewers, 1" apart.
- Cook the tikkas in a hot tandoor or grill under a medium
  hot gas or electric grill as described on pp. xiv–xv for 5–6
  minutes.
- Baste with oil, turn the skewers and grill again for another
  3–4 minutes, till the juices run clear when the flesh is pierced
  with a fork.
- Slip the tikkas off the skewers on to a serving platter.
- Sprinkle chaat masala powder on top and serve as a starter
  with onion rings and mint chutney (p. 12) on the side.

MACHCHI TIKKA MASALA

Makes 2–3

Now, make the fish tikka masala using this recipe.

Sole fish, boneless 500 gm
Lime juice 1 tbsp
Coriander leaves, fresh, chopped 1 tbsp

Tikka masala
Oil 2 tbsp
Onion, chopped 1
Ginger paste 1 tbsp
Garlic paste 1 tbsp
Turmeric powder 1 tsp
Red chilli powder 1 tsp
Cumin powder 1 tsp
Coriander powder 1 tsp
Garam masala powder 1 tsp
Salt 1 tsp
Green chillies, chopped fine 2
Tomato purée 1½ cups
Lime juice 1 tsp
Butter 2½ tbsp
Cream, fresh ½ cup

- Wash the fish and pat dry with paper towels. Cut it into 2" cubes.
- Rub with 1 tbsp of lime juice, rinse and pat dry again.
- Heat the oil in a pan. Add the onion and sauté on medium heat, till golden brown.
- Mix in the ginger and garlic and stir for 2–3 minutes
- Add the spice powders and salt and sauté, till fragrant.

Sprinkle in some water, if required to prevent it from sticking to the pan.
- Add the fish cubes and sauté on low to medium heat for 4–5 minutes.
- Mix in the green chillies, tomato purée and lime juice and stir for about 4 minutes.
- Add the butter and stir till it melts.
- Stir in the cream and remove from heat.
- Serve hot sprinkled with coriander leaves.

TAMARIND FISH KEBABS

IMLI MACHCHI TIKKA

Makes 2

Just imagine a tangy grilled fish. This recipe is my wife's favourite—fish tikka with a hint of sweet and sour.

Sole fish, boneless 350 gm
Oil, for basting 2 tbsp

Tamarind paste
Tamarind, without seeds and fibre 3½ tbsp
Jaggery, grated ½ tbsp
Red chilli powder 1 tsp
Cumin powder ½ tsp
Garam masala powder ½ tsp
Salt 1 tsp

First marinade
White vinegar 2 tsp
White pepper powder ½ tsp
Salt ½ tsp

Second marinade
Yogurt, hung, whisked ½ cup (p. 5)
Red chilli powder ½ tsp
Asafoetida powder ¼ tsp
Green cardamom powder ½ tsp

- Wash the fish and pat dry with paper towels. Cut it into 2" cubes.

Tamarind paste
- Combine the ingredients for the tamarind paste in a pan with ½ cup of water.
- Put the pan over low to medium heat and stir, till the tamarind dissolves and the paste is well blended.
- Remove from heat and strain into a bowl. Set aside.

First marination

- Combine the ingredients for the first marinade in a bowl and whisk, till they blend well.
- Add the fish and mix well, to ensure that it is completely coated with the marinade.
- Cover and set aside to marinate in the refrigerator for 30 minutes.

Second marination

- Combine the ingredients for the second marinade with the tamarind paste in another bowl and whisk, till they blend well.
- Remove excess moisture from the marinated fish and add the fish cubes to the bowl.
- Mix well, to ensure that they are completely coated with the second marinade.
- Cover and set aside to marinate in the refrigerator for 2–4 hours.

For the tikkas

- Remove the fish from the refrigerator and bring to room temperature.
- Thread the fish on to long, thin metal skewers, 1" apart.
- Cook the tikka in a medium-hot tandoor or grill under a very hot gas or electric grill as described on pp. xiv–xv for about 8 minutes.
- Baste with oil, turn the skewers and grill again for another 3–4 minutes.
- Slip the kebabs off the skewers on to a serving platter and serve hot with mint chutney (p. 12).

VARIATION:

Tamarind Paneer Tikka: Use paneer (p. 5) in place of the fish and cut it into 1½" cubes. Cook it in the same way.

FENUGREEK FISH KEBABS

METHI MACHCHI TIKKA

Makes 2

This is a very popular Punjabi recipe as the Punjabis enjoy and relish fenugreek.

Sole fish, boneless, minced 200 gm
Cheese spread, commercial 2 tsp
Egg, whisked 1
Ginger paste 1 tsp
Garlic paste 1 tsp
Coriander leaves, fresh, chopped fine 1½ tsp
Green chillies, seeded, chopped fine 1 tsp
Fenugreek leaves, fresh, chopped fine 4 tsp
Carom seeds ½ tsp
Cumin powder 1 tsp
Asafoetida powder ¼ tsp
White pepper powder 1 tsp
Salt 1½ tsp
Butter, melted, for basting 2 tbsp

- Squeeze out extra moisture from the mince. Put the mince into a bowl.
- Add the remaining ingredients for the kebabs and mix well with your hands.
- Cover and set aside in the refrigerator for 2–3 hours.
- Remove the kebab mix from the refrigerator and bring to room temperature.
- Wet your hands and a few long, thick metal skewers.
- Roll the kebab mix into 4 balls and thread them on to the skewers. Shape the balls into 2"-long kebabs along the length of the skewers, 1" apart.
- Grill the kebabs under a hot gas or electric grill as described on pp. xiv–xv for 6–7 minutes.

- Baste with melted butter, turn the skewers and grill again for another 3–4 minutes.
- Slip the kebabs off the skewers on to a serving platter.
- Serve hot with a salad and any dip of your choice.

MINTED FISH KEBABS
PUDINA MACHHLI TIKKA

Makes 5–6

This is a fine dish with a hint of fresh mint. Indeed a good appetizer.

River sole, boneless 1 kg
Butter, melted, for basting 4 tbsp
Parsley, fresh, chopped 1 tsp

First marinade
Ginger paste 1 tbsp
Garlic paste 2 tbsp
Lime juice 3 tbsp
Red chilli powder 1 tsp
Salt 1 tsp

Second marinade
Yogurt, hung, whisked 1½ cups (p. 5)
Oil 3 tbsp
Green chillies, seeded, chopped 2 tbsp
Coriander leaves, fresh, chopped 4 tbsp
Mint leaves, puréed 4–5 tsp
Curry leaves, fresh 1 tbsp
Onion, chopped 1
Pomegranate seeds, dried, crushed 2 tsp
Dried mango powder 2 tbsp
Carom seeds 1 tsp
Cornflour 2 tbsp
Gram flour, roasted 2 tbsp
Garam masala powder 1 tsp
Black pepper powder 1 tsp
Cinnamon powder 1 tsp
Salt 3 tsp

- Wash the fish and pat dry with paper towels. Cut it into 2" cubes.

First marination
- Combine the ingredients for the first marinade in a bowl and whisk till it blends well.
- Add the fish and mix well, to ensure that it is completely coated with the marinade.
- Cover and set aside to marinate in the refrigerator for 30 minutes.

Second marination
- Whisk the yogurt with the remaining ingredients for the second marinade in another bowl, till they blend well.
- Drain the marinated fish pieces and add them to the bowl.
- Mix well, to ensure that they are completely coated with the second marinade.
- Cover and set aside to marinate in the refrigerator for 3–4 hours.

For the kebabs
- Remove the fish from the refrigerator and bring to room temperature.
- Thread the fish on to long, thin metal skewers, 1" apart.
- Cook the kebabs in a medium-hot tandoor or grill under a medium hot gas or electric grill as described on pp. xiv–xv for 6–7 minutes.
- Baste with melted butter, turn the skewers and grill again for another 3–4 minutes.
- Slip the kebabs off the skewers on to a serving platter. Sprinkle parsley on top and serve hot.

SALMON BASIL TIKKA

Makes 2

Pink salmon is a delicacy anywhere in the world, and basil imparts an awesome flavour to grilled fish. I was once invited to Stockholm by an international celebrity chef to experiment with Indo-Swedish cuisine. Venison is very popular in Sweden, so we marinated the tender venison with Indian spices and yoghurt, grilled it and served it with basil and thyme sauce. On my return to India, I invited some guests and served salmon marinated with puréed basil and other condiments. The result was outstanding.

Pink salmon, boneless 250 gm
Butter, melted 1½ tbsp

First marinade
Ginger paste 1 tsp
Garlic paste 1 tsp
Basil leaves, fresh, puréed 1 tsp
Lime juice 1 tsp
Salt 1 tsp

Second marinade
Yogurt, hung, whisked 4 tbsp (p. 5)
Lime juice 1 tsp
Olive oil 1 tsp
Gram flour 1 tsp
Coriander powder ½ tsp
Cumin powder 1 tsp
White pepper powder 1 tsp
Salt 1½ tsp

- Wash the fish and pat dry with paper towels. Cut it into 8 cubes.

First marination

- Combine the ingredients for the first marinade in a bowl and whisk till they blend well.
- Add the fish and mix well, to ensure that it is completely coated with the marinade.
- Cover and set aside to marinate in the refrigerator for 30 minutes.

Second marination

- Whisk the yogurt with the remaining ingredients for the second marinade in another bowl, till they blend well.
- Drain the marinated fish and add it to the bowl.
- Mix well, to ensure that it is completely coated with the second marinade.
- Cover and set aside to marinate in the refrigerator for 2–3 hours.

For the tikkas

- Remove the fish from the refrigerator and bring to room temperature.
- Thread the fish on to long, thin metal skewers, 1" apart.
- Cook the tikka in a medium-hot tandoor or grill under a hot gas or electric grill as described on pp. xiv–xv for 6–7 minutes.
- Baste with melted butter, turn the skewers and grill again for another 3–4 minutes.
- Slip the fish off the skewers on to a serving platter and serve hot.

TURKISH FISH KEBABS

KEBAB-E-OZUNBORUN

Makes 8–10

This is a special Turkish recipe. I was visiting Turkey in the winter of 2011, when I was invited by a restaurateur to an old fish market. I was totally enamoured to see restaurants on both sides of a narrow street, brightly lit, with traditional gypsy musicians playing their instruments and singing by the table sides. This fish was highly recommended by the chef. Here is my take on the special fish kebab.

Salmon, boneless 1½ kg
Parsley, fresh, chopped 1 tsp

Marinade
Lime juice 200 ml
White vinegar 1 tbsp
Onions, medium-sized, grated 2
Mustard powder ½ tsp
Red chilli powder 1 tsp
Black pepper, freshly ground 2 tsp
Salt 3 tsp

Basting sauce
Butter, unsalted, melted 4 tbsp
Lime juice 3 tbsp
Tomato paste 3 tbsp

- Wash the fish and pat dry with paper towels. Cut it into 1" cubes.

Marination
- Combine the ingredients for the marinade in a bowl and whisk, till they blend well.

- Add the fish and mix well, to ensure that it is completely coated with the marinade.
- Cover and set aside to marinate in the refrigerator overnight.

Basting sauce
- Put the ingredients for the basting sauce in a pan. Bring to a boil and remove from heat.
- Set aside, till cool.

For the kebabs
- Remove the fish from the refrigerator and bring to room temperature.
- Thread the fish on to long, thin metal skewers, 1" apart.
- Grill the kebabs over a charcoal fire or under a hot gas or electric grill as described on pp. xiv–xv for 4–5 minutes.
- Brush with the basting sauce, turn the skewers and grill again for another 4–5 minutes.
- Slip the kebabs off the skewers on to a serving platter. Sprinkle parsley on top and serve hot with a garlic dip.

TANDOORI PRAWNS

Makes 5

Tandoori prawns are very popular in India and the trend is catching up in the West, too. Grilled prawns were always popular in the West, but when tandoori prawns are served there at a catered party, it is amazing to observe how people make a bee line for them.

Prawns, king-sized 10
Butter, melted for basting

Marinade
Yogurt, hung, whisked 2½ cups (p. 5)
Egg, whisked 1
Cream, fresh 4 tbsp
Ginger, chopped fine 2 tsp
Ginger paste 1 tbsp
Garlic paste 1½ tbsp
Onion, chopped fine 2 tbsp
Coriander leaves, fresh, chopped fine 2 tsp
Mint leaves, fresh, chopped fine 2 tsp
Fenugreek seeds, powdered 1 tsp
Red chilli powder 1 tsp
Garam masala powder 1 tsp
Cinnamon powder ½ tsp
Salt to taste

- Shell the prawns, leaving the tails intact. Remove the veins and wash the prawns thoroughly. Pat dry with paper towels.

Marination
- Combine all the ingredients for the marinade in a bowl and whisk, till they blend well.

- Add the prawns and mix well, to ensure that they are completely coated with the marinade.
- Cover and set aside to marinate in the refrigerator for 4–5 hour.

For the prawns
- Remove the prawns from the refrigerator and bring to room temperature.
- Thread the prawns horizontally on to long, thin metal skewers, 1" apart.
- Cook the kebabs in a medium-hot tandoor or grill under a hot gas or electric grill as described on pp. xiv–xv for 8–10 minutes.
- Baste with melted butter, turn the skewers and grill again for another 3–4 minutes.
- Slip the prawns off the skewers on to a serving platter.
- Serve hot with a salad and mint chutney (p. 12).

THAI CHILLI TANDOORI PRAWNS

Makes 2

I am always inspired by Thai food to create new dishes. One such experiment resulted in this delicious fusion recipe.

Prawns, king-sized 250 gm
Ghee, melted, for basting 2 tbsp
Parsley, fresh, chopped 1 tsp

First marinade
Ginger paste ½ tsp
Garlic paste 1 tsp
White vinegar 1 tsp
Red chilli powder ½ tsp
Salt 1 tsp

Second marinade
Yogurt, hung, whisked 3 tbsp (p. 5)
Ginger paste 1 tsp
Garlic paste 1 tsp
Lime juice 1 tsp
Soy sauce ½ tsp
Red chilli paste 2 tsp
Cornflour 2 tsp
Cumin powder 1 tsp
Mustard powder 1 tsp
Salt 2 tsp

- Shell the prawns, leaving the tails intact. Remove the veins and wash the prawns thoroughly. Pat dry with paper towels.

First marination
- Combine the ingredients for the first marinade in a bowl and whisk, till they blend well.

- Add the prawns and mix well, to ensure that they are completely coated with the marinade.
- Cover and set aside to marinate in the refrigerator for 30 minutes.

Second marination
- Whisk the yogurt with the remaining ingredients for the second marinade in another bowl.
- Drain the marinated prawns and add them to the bowl.
- Mix well, to ensure that they are completely coated with the second marinade.
- Cover and set aside to marinate in the refrigerator for 4–5 hours.

For the prawns
- Remove the prawns from the refrigerator and bring to room temperature.
- Thread the prawns horizontally on to long, thin metal skewers, 1" apart.
- Brush with leftover marinade.
- Cook the prawns in a medium-hot tandoor or grill under a hot gas or electric grill as described on pp. xiv–xv for 6–7 minutes.
- Baste with melted ghee, turn the skewers and grill again for another 4–5 minutes.
- Slip the prawns off the skewers on to a serving platter. Sprinkle parsley on top and serve hot with garlic flatbread (p. 31) and a green salad.

GARLIC CHILLI PRAWN KEBABS

Makes 6

A deadly combination of chilli and garlic makes this prawn kebab recipe just irresistible. This makes a great appetizer when you have a small dinner or a party at home. Mildly spiced with a hint of garlicky flavour have this kebab with a crisp garlic bread and chillies to tantalize your taste buds.

Prawns, king-sized 12
Lime, cut into wedges 2

Marinade
Olive oil, extra virgin 2 tbsp
Lime juice 1 tbsp
Garlic, chopped fine 3 cloves
Red chilli, fresh, seeded, chopped fine 1
Coriander leaves, fresh, chopped 2 tsp
Red chilli, dried, coarsely ground 1
Coriander powder 1 tsp
Black pepper, coarsely crushed 1 tsp
Salt 2½ tsp

- Shell the prawns, leaving the tails intact. Remove the veins and wash the prawns thoroughly. Pat dry with paper towels.

Marination
- Combine the ingredients for the marinade in a bowl and whisk till well blended.
- Add the prawns and mix well, to ensure that they are completely coated with the marinade.
- Cover and set aside to marinate in the refrigerator for 2–3 hours.

For the kebabs

- Remove the prawns from the refrigerator and bring to room temperature.
- Thread the prawns horizontally on to long, thin metal skewers, 1" apart.
- Grill the prawns under a very hot gas or electric grill as described on pp. xiv–xv for 2–3 minutes.
- Baste with the leftover marinade, turn the skewers and grill again for another 2–3 minutes.
- Slip the kebabs off the skewers on to a serving platter and serve with lime wedges, garlic flatbread (p. 31) and mango chutney (p. 13) or a garlic dip on the side.

COCONUT PRAWN KEBABS

Makes 10–12

I have always enjoyed the tropical flavour of fresh coconut in drinks as well as in food. I experimented with prawns marinated in coconut milk and the result was delicious. I recommend trying the same marinade with vegetables or other meats as well.

Tiger prawns 10
Butter, melted 2 tbsp
Lime, cut into wedges 2
Parsley, fresh, chopped 2 tsp

Marinade
Ginger, julienned 1" piece
Garlic, crushed 1 clove
Coconut, fresh, grated 2 tsp
Lemon grass, roughly chopped 1 stalk
Coriander powder 1 tsp
White pepper powder 1 tsp
Salt 1½ tsp
Coconut milk 1 cup

• Shell the prawns, leaving the tails intact. Remove the veins and wash the prawns thoroughly. Pat dry with paper towels.

Marination
• Put the ingredients for the marinade, except the coconut milk, into a pan and place on low heat.
• When the mixture starts simmering, remove from heat and set aside for 25–30 minutes for the flavours to infuse.
• Strain and mix in the prawns. Add coconut milk.
• Cover and set aside to marinate in the refrigerator for 3–4 hours.

For the kebabs

- Soak bamboo skewers in water for 20 minutes and drain.
- Remove the prawns from the refrigerator and bring to room temperature.
- Thread each prawn horizontally on to a drained bamboo skewer, tail end first.
- Brush liberally with leftover marinade.
- Grill the prawns under a hot gas or electric grill as described on pp. xiv–xv for 2–3 minutes.
- Baste with melted butter, turn the skewers and grill again for another 2–3 minutes, till the prawns turn pink and are just cooked.
- Slip the prawns off the skewers on to a serving platter. Garnish with parsley and serve hot with lime wedges and a fresh green salad.

PRAWN KEBABS WITH MANGO CHILLI SALSA

Makes 2

This recipe is inspired by my most memorable trip to Rio. I was on the beach at a salsa restaurant which had a unique menu and served a variety of salsas with almost every dish. And of course the salsa dancers were on the stage while the salsa-based food sang its way down to the tummy.

Tiger prawns 4
Olive oil, for basting 1 tbsp

Marinade
Olive oil 1 tbsp
Ginger paste 1 tsp
Garlic, chopped fine 1 clove
Lime juice ½ tsp
Red chilli, fresh, seeded, chopped fine 1
Salt 1 tsp

Salsa
Mango, ripe, peeled, chopped ½
Coriander leaves, fresh, chopped 3 tbsp
Parsley, fresh, chopped 1 tsp
Red chillies, dried, coarsely ground 1 tsp
Cumin seeds ½ tsp
Dry sherry 1 tsp
Olive oil 1 tbsp
Honey 1 tbsp
Black pepper, freshly ground 1 tsp
Salt 1 tsp

- Shell the prawns, leaving the tails intact. Remove the veins and wash the prawns thoroughly. Pat dry with paper towels.

Marination

- Combine the ingredients for the marinade in a bowl and whisk till they blend well.
- Add the prawns and mix well, to ensure that they are completely coated with the marinade.
- Cover and set aside to marinate in the refrigerator for 2–3 hours.

For the kebabs

- Remove the prawns from the refrigerator and bring to room temperature.
- Thread the prawns horizontally on to long, thin metal skewers, 1" apart.
- Grill the prawns under a medium-hot gas or electric grill as described on pp. xiv–xv for 3–4 minutes.
- Baste with olive oil, turn the skewers and grill again for another 4–5 minutes.
- Combine the ingredients for the salsa in a bowl and mix well.
- Slip the prawns off the skewer on to a serving platter and spoon the mango-chilli salsa alongside.

TANGY THAI PRAWN KEBABS

Makes 3

When caterers serve prawns on the menu the price of the menu is bound to go up as prawns are an expensive delicacy. I remember this was one of the special recipes at our banquets and whenever guests chose this dish my banquet manager would always remind them that the cost of catering would go up. But everyone would love this tangy prawn dish at parties.

Tiger prawns 6
Pita bread 3 pieces (p. 24)
Lettuce, shredded ½ cup
Sour cream ¼ cup

Marinade
Garlic, crushed 1 clove
Honey 2½ tbsp
White vinegar 1 tsp
Sesame seed oil 1 tsp
Soy sauce 2 tbsp
Mustard powder 1 tsp
Coriander powder 1 tsp
Sea salt 2 tsp

Vegetables
White onion ½
Red onion 1
Red bell pepper 1
Zucchini ½ cup
Mushroom caps, kept whole ½ cup

- Shell the prawns, leaving the tails intact. Remove the veins and wash the prawns thoroughly. Pat dry with paper towels.

Marination

- Put the honey in a bowl and add the prawns. Mix well.
- Cover and set aside in the refrigerator for 1 hour.
- Combine the remaining ingredients for the marinade in a small bowl and mix well.
- Add to the prawns and mix well, to ensure that they are completely coated with the marinade.
- Cover and set aside to marinate in the refrigerator for 1 hour

Vegetables

- Cut the onion into quarters and open out the layers.
- Cut the bell pepper into squares and zucchini into cubes.
- Leave the mushroom caps whole.

For the prawns and vegetables

- Remove the prawns from the refrigerator and bring to room temperature.
- Thread the prawns and vegetables alternately on to long, thin metal skewers, 1" apart.
- Grill under a medium-hot gas or electric grill as described on pp. xiv–xv for 15 minutes or till the edges of the vegetables start browning.
- Baste with the leftover marinade, turn the skewers and grill again for another 4–5 minutes.
- Cut the pita bread into half. Spread sour cream inside and fill with prawns and vegetables. Sprinkle lettuce on top and serve hot with mango chutney (p. 13).

PRAWN KEBABS
WITH PESTO SAUCE

Makes 5

This recipe is inspired by an Italian dish I tasted at a fancy bistro in Venice. They served the pasta with pesto sauce. I ventured to marinate prawns with fresh, home-made pesto sauce.

Pesto Sauce
Garlic 2 cloves
Basil leaves, fresh 1 cup
Pine nuts 1½ tbsp
Olive oil, extra virgin ¼ cup
Parmesan cheese, grated ¼ cup
Black pepper, freshly ground ¼ tsp
Salt ¼ tsp

Kebabs
Tiger prawns 10
Cream, fresh ½ cup
Onion 1
Red bell pepper 1
Yellow bell pepper 1

Pesto sauce
- Put the garlic in a food processor and mince.
- Add the remaining ingredients and blend, till puréed.
- Transfer to a glass jar and refrigerate, till required.

Kebabs
- Shell the prawns, leaving the tails intact. Remove the veins and wash the prawns thoroughly. Pat dry with paper towels.

Marination
- Whisk the pesto sauce and cream in a bowl.

- Add the prawns and mix well, to ensure that they are completely coated with the marinade.
- Cover and set aside to marinate in the refrigerator for 3 hours.

Vegetables
- Cut the onion into quarters and open out the layers.
- Cut the bell peppers into squares.

For the prawns and vegetables
- Remove the prawns from the refrigerator and bring to room temperature.
- Thread the prawns and vegetables alternately on to long, thin metal skewers, 1" apart.
- Grill under a medium-hot gas or electric grill as described on pp. xiv–xv for 3–4 minutes or till the edges of the vegetables start browning.
- Baste with the leftover marinade, turn the skewers and grill again for another 2–3 minutes.
- Slip the prawns and vegetables off the skewers on to a serving platter and serve hot.

CRAB AND PRAWN KEBABS

Makes 2

- This is a unique recipe for a kebab with a blend of crab and prawn meat, resulting in a wonderful seafood fusion.

Crab meat 100 gm
Prawn meat 100 gm
Ghee, for basting 2 tbsp
Parsley, fresh, chopped 1 tsp

First marinade
Ginger paste 1 tsp
Garlic paste 1 tsp
White vinegar ½ tsp
Red chilli powder 1 tsp
Salt 1 tsp

Second marinade
Cheese spread, commercial 3 tsp
Green chillies, chopped fine ½ tsp
Coriander leaves, fresh, chopped fine 1 tsp
Mint leaves, fresh, chopped 1 tsp
Green cardamom powder ¼ tsp
Ginger, dried, powdered ½ tsp
Pomegranate seeds, dried, crushed 1 tsp
White pepper powder 1 tsp

- Wash the crab and prawn meat and pat dry with paper towels. Chop coarsely.

First marination
- Combine the ingredients for the marinade in a bowl and whisk, till they blend well.
- Add the crab and prawn meat and mix, till they blend well.

- Cover and set aside to marinate in the refrigerator for 30 minutes.

Second marination
- Add the ingredients for the second marinade to the same bowl. Mix till they blend well.
- Cover and set aside in the refrigerator for 3–4 hours.

For the kebabs
- Remove the kebab mix from the refrigerator and bring to room temperature.
- Wet your hands and a few long, thick metal skewers.
- Roll the kebab mix into 4 balls and thread them on to the skewers. Shape the balls into 2"-long kebabs along the length of the skewers, 1" apart.
- Cook the kebabs in a medium-hot tandoor or grill under a hot gas or electric grill as described on pp. xiv–xv for 6–7 minutes.
- Baste with melted ghee, turn the skewers and grill again for another 3–4 minutes.
- Slip the kebabs off the skewers on to a serving platter. Sprinkle parsley on top and serve hot with a salad and any dip of choice.

SHRIMP AND STEAK KEBABS

Makes 6–8

This is a special two-in-one recipe to satisfy those who love both seafood and beef. These mildly spiced kebabs with barbecued veggies taste awesome. This has an interesting story behind it. Once I was to compete in a food show where the chefs had to prepare a dish from the raw materials provided at the competition venue. I happened to find out that between the two judges one preferred beef and the other was a seafood lover. So it is a no-brainer why I invented this one.

Beef sirloin steak 750 gm
Shrimp, large-sized 12
Mushrooms, kept whole 250 gm
Red bell peppers, quartered 3
Butter, melted, for basting ¼ cup
Coriander leaves, fresh, chopped 1 tbsp
Lime, cut into wedges 1

Marinade
White wine 3 tbsp
Mustard powder ½ tsp
Cumin powder 1 tsp
Black pepper, freshly ground 1½ tsp
Salt 2½ tsp

- Wash the steak and pat dry with paper towels. Cut it into 1½" cubes.
- Shell the shrimp, remove the veins and wash thoroughly. Pat dry.
- Clean the mushrooms and keep whole.

Marination
- Combine the ingredients for the marinade in a bowl and whisk, till they blend well.

- Add the steak, shrimp, mushrooms and bell peppers and mix well, to ensure that they are completely coated with the marinade.
- Cover and set aside to marinate in the refrigerator overnight.

For the kebabs
- Remove the steak, shrimp, mushrooms and bell peppers from the refrigerator and bring to room temperature.
- Thread 3 steak cubes, 3 shrimp, 3 mushrooms and 3 bell pepper pieces alternately on to long, thin metal skewers, 1" apart.
- Grill the kebabs under a very hot gas or electric grill as described on pp. xiv–xv for 7–8 minutes.
- Baste with melted butter, turn the skewers and grill again for another 8–10 minutes.
- Slip the kebabs off the skewers on to a serving platter. Sprinkle coriander leaves on top and serve hot with lime wedges and pickled vegetables.

TANDOORI LOBSTER

Makes 4

In 1999, when I was doing the spade work to give a new look to Moti Mahal in terms of menu and contemporary interiors, this was one of the high-end recipes I included in the menu of the Moti Mahal Tandoori Trail outlets.

Lobsters, medium-sized 4
Oil, hot, for coating the shells
Butter, melted, for basting ½ cup

First marinade
Ginger paste 4 tsp
Garlic paste 4 tsp
Carom seeds ½ tsp
Malt vinegar ½ cup
Salt 3 tsp

Second marinade
Yogurt, hung, whisked 1 cup (p. 5)
Egg, whisked 1
Paneer, grated 4 tbsp (p. 5)
Oil 4 tbsp
Red chilli paste 1 tsp
Gram flour 3 tbsp
Coriander powder 1 tsp
White pepper powder 1 tsp

- Cut each lobster into half, then shell and clean the flesh. Cut the flesh into 1" cubes.
- Wash well and pat dry with paper towels.
- Wash the shells and dry them. Dip them in hot oil. Drain and set aside.

First marination
- Combine the ingredients for the first marinade in a bowl and whisk well.
- Add the lobster pieces and mix well, to ensure that they are completely coated with the marinade.
- Cover and set aside to marinate in the refrigerator for 1 hour.

Second marination
- Whisk the yogurt with the remaining ingredients for the second marinade in another bowl.
- Add the marinated lobster pieces and mix well, to ensure that they are completely coated with the second marinade.
- Cover and set aside to marinate in the refrigerator for 6–8 hours.

For the lobster
- Remove the lobster from the refrigerator and bring to room temperature.
- Thread the lobster on to long, thin metal skewers, 1" apart.
- Cook the lobster in a medium-hot tandoor or grill under a hot gas or electric grill as described on pp. xiv–xv for about 5 minutes.
- Baste with melted butter, turn the skewers and grill again for another 2–3 minutes.
- Put the lobster flesh into their shells.
- Serve hot with lettuce, tomato slices and onion rings on the side.

~

ASPARAGUS KEBABS

Makes 2

A rather unique, contemporary recipe; I made it at a fusion cooking show in Germany.

Fresh green asparagus spears 250 gm
Oil, for frying ¼ cup
Parsley, fresh, chopped 1 tsp

Filling
Coriander leaves, fresh, chopped 2 tbsp
Dried mango powder ½ tsp

Coating
Green peas, shelled ¼ cup
Oil 2 tbsp
Cumin seeds 1 tsp
Ginger paste 2 tsp
Garlic paste 2 tsp
Green chillies, chopped fine 5
Coriander powder 2 tsp
Cumin powder 1 tsp
Gram flour 3 tbsp
Paneer, crumbled,made from 1 litre of milk (p. 5)
Mustard powder ½ tsp
Chaat masala powder ½ tsp
Garam masala powder 1 tsp
Castor sugar ½ tsp
Salt 2 tsp
Lime juice 3 tsp

- Scrape the asparagus spears and blanch in plenty of boiling salted water for 5 minutes. Drain and plunge into a bowl of cold water. Drain.

Filling
- Slice off the tips and place in a bowl with the ingredients for the filling. Set aside.
- Chop the asparagus stalks roughly and purée them in a blender. Set aside.

Coating
- Wash the green peas in warm water and purée them in a blender. Set aside.
- Heat 2 tbsp of oil in a pan. Add the cumin seeds and sauté on medium heat for a few seconds.
- Add ginger and garlic and sauté for 1½ minutes.
- Stir in the green chillies, coriander powder and cumin powder and sauté for a few seconds.
- Reduce heat to low and add the gram flour. Sauté for a few seconds, till the raw aroma of the gram flour disappears.
- Mix in the puréed asparagus and green peas. Sauté for 10–15 minutes on low heat, till it becomes paste-like.
- Remove from heat and add paneer.
- Sprinkle in the remaining coating ingredients and mix thoroughly.
- When cool, knead gently, to make a soft dough.

To shape the kebabs
- Wet your hands and divide the filling and dough into 12 equal portions.
- Roll the dough into balls and flatten them slightly between your palms.
- Put a portion of filling in the centre of a flattened ball and pull the edges up to cover the filling completely.
- Shape into a ball and flatten it slightly to form a round patty.
- Make all the kebabs in the same way.

- Put the kebabs in the refrigerator to firm up for at least 30 minutes.

To cook the kebabs
- Heat the oil in a non-stick frying pan. Shallow-fry the kebabs on medium heat, on both sides, till evenly cooked and crisp.
- Drain on kitchen paper.
- Arrange the kebabs on a serving platter and sprinkle parsley on top. Serve hot with mint chutney (p. 12) or a cheese dip.

RED KIDNEY BEAN KEBABS

Makes 3–4

This recipe is dedicated to all the children who love eating rajma-chawal (red kidney beans with rice), as I made this dish for my son who would insist on eating red beans at every meal.

Red kidney beans 1 cup
Ginger, chopped 1"
Garlic, chopped 4 cloves
Coriander leaves, fresh, chopped 2 tsp
Potato, small, boiled, grated 1
Cornflour 1 tsp
Red chilli powder ½ tsp
Dried mango powder 1 tsp
Garam masala powder ½ tsp
Cinnamon powder ⅓ tsp
Green cardamom powder 1 tsp
Mace powder ⅓ tsp
Black pepper powder ⅓ tsp
Salt 1 tsp
Ghee for shallow-frying ¼ cup
Chaat masala powder 1 tsp

To smoke the kebab mix
Charcoal, red-hot 1 piece
Cloves 3
Asafoetida, kept whole ½" piece
Ghee ½ tsp

- Wash the beans and soak overnight in water.
- Drain and rinse the beans thoroughly.
- Boil the beans with the ginger, garlic and salt, till tender.
- Drain the water and set the beans aside, till cool.
- Grind the beans in a blender to make a fine paste.

- Transfer to a bowl and mix in the remaining ingredients for the kebabs.
- Knead, till well blended.

To smoke the kebab mix
- Smoke the kebab mix as given on p. 44, adding the asafoetida piece with the cloves and ghee.

To cook the kebabs
- Grease your hands lightly and divide the kebab mix into 6 equal portions. Shape into balls and flatten them slightly to form round patties.
- Heat the ghee in a non-stick frying pan and shallow-fry the kebabs, till light golden-brown on both sides.
- Drain on kitchen paper.
- Arrange the kebabs on a serving platter.
- Sprinkle chaat masala powder on top and serve hot with mint chutney (p. 12).

WHITE BEAN KEBABS

Makes 3–4

A vegetarian version of the famous Lucknowi kebabs; a real treat!

White kidney beans 1 cup
Ginger-garlic paste 1 tsp
Poppy seed paste 1 tsp
Fenugreek seed powder 1 tsp
Cumin powder ½ tsp
Dried mango powder 1 tsp
Garam masala powder 1 tsp
Cinnamon powder ⅓ tsp
Green cardamom powder 1 tsp
Mace powder ⅓ tsp
Black pepper powder ⅓ tsp
Salt 1 tsp
Ghee for shallow-frying ¼ cup
Chaat masala powder 1 tsp

To smoke the kebab mix
Charcoal, red-hot 1 piece
Cloves 3
Asafoetida powder ¼ tsp
Ghee ½ tsp

- Wash the beans and soak in warm water for 6–8 hours.
- Drain the beans and rinse thoroughly.
- Boil the beans on high heat, till tender.
- Drain and cool.
- Grind the beans in a blender to make a fine paste.
- Transfer to a bowl and mix in the remaining ingredients for the kebabs. Knead, till they blend well.

To smoke the kebab mix

- Smoke the kebab mix as given on p. 44, adding the asafoetida powder with the cloves and ghee.

To cook the kebabs

- Grease your hands lightly and divide the kebab mix into 6 equal portions.
- Roll into balls and flatten them slightly to form round patties.
- Heat the ghee in a non-stick frying pan and shallow-fry the kebabs, till light golden-brown on both sides.
- Drain on kitchen paper.
- Arrange the kebabs on a serving platter.
- Sprinkle chaat masala powder on top and serve hot with mint chutney (p. 12) or sesame tomato chutney (p. 14).

BENGAL GRAM KEBABS

Makes 3–4

My grandmother insisted on cooking certain dishes on certain days of the week as a ritual owing to some superstitions. For instance, we always had whole Bengal gram (kala chana) curry and rice on Saturdays. I would argue with her about why we must have predictable meals. And even if we had to use a particular ingredient, why not try a different recipe? So on one Saturday, she created this unusual dish using whole Bengal gram instead of the regular curry.

Whole Bengal gram/kala chana I cup
Ginger 1" piece
Garlic cloves 4
Salt 1 tsp
Paneer, grated 2½ tbsp (p. 5)
Potato, boiled, mashed 4 tbsp
Coriander leaves, fresh, chopped 1 tsp
Cornflour 2 tsp
Red chilli powder 1 tsp
Coriander powder ½ tsp
Asafoetida powder ½ tsp
Dried mango powder 1 tsp
Garam masala powder 1 tsp
Breadcrumbs, fresh 2 tbsp
Oil for frying ¼ cup

- Wash the gram and soak it in water for 2 hours.
- Drain the gram, rinse and boil in water with the ginger, garlic and salt, till tender.
- Drain water and set the gram aside, till cool.
- Grind the gram in a blender to make a fine paste.
- Transfer to a bowl and mix in the remaining ingredients for the kebabs.

- Place in the refrigerator for 3–4 hours, to firm up.
- Grease your hands lightly and divide the kebab mix into 6 equal portions. Shape into balls and flatten them slightly to form round patties.
- Spread the breadcrumbs on a plate. Press the kebabs into the breadcrumbs, to coat completely.
- Heat oil in a non-stick frying pan and shallow-fry the kebabs, till light golden-brown on both sides.
- Drain on kitchen paper.
- Serve hot with mint chutney (p. 12) and pita bread (p. 24).

BOTTLE GOURD KEBABS

Makes 2-3

I always enjoy eating these when I want a light meal. The flavour is delicate and the result mouth-watering.

Bottle gourd/lauki 500 gm
Salt 2 tsp
Garlic 3 cloves
Spinach 4 tbsp
Paneer, grated 1 cup (p. 5)
Ginger, chopped 3 tsp
Onions, medium-sized, chopped 2
Green peas, shelled, boiled ¼ cup
Green chillies, chopped 2
Coriander leaves, fresh, chopped 2 tbsp
Cumin powder ½ tsp
Dried mango powder 1 tsp
Green cardamom powder ½ tsp
Breadcrumbs, fresh 3 tbsp
Oil for shallow frying
Coriander leaves, fresh, chopped 1 tbsp
Lime, cut into wedges 1

- Peel the gourd and chop it roughly.
- Transfer to a pan and add a pinch of salt and just enough water to cover.
- Cook on medium heat, till tender. Drain and refresh in cold water.
- Drain the gourd thoroughly and put it in a bowl.
- Squeeze out the juice from the garlic and blend with the spinach, till smooth.
- Add to the bowl containing the gourd with the remaining ingredients for the kebabs.
- Mix thoroughly, till it blends well.

- Put the kebab mix in the refrigerator to firm up for at least 1 hour.

For the kebabs
- Remove the kebab mix from the refrigerator and bring to room temperature.
- Divide the kebab mix into 6 equal portions and roll them into balls. Flatten them slightly to form round patties.
- Heat the oil in a non-stick frying pan and shallow-fry the patties on both sides, till evenly cooked and golden brown.
- Drain on kitchen paper.
- Arrange the kebabs on a serving platter and sprinkle coriander leaves on top. Serve hot with lime wedges and sesame tomato chutney (p. 14).

MINTED TANDOORI CAULIFLOWER

Makes 6–8

Cauliflower is a wonderful vegetable; one can have it as a salad, starter or main course. When marinated with a hint of mint and grilled, the result is divine.

Cauliflowers, medium-sized, kept whole 4
Salt 2 tsp
Green cardamoms 3
Cinnamon 1" stick
Cloves 4
Black peppercorns 5
Oil, for basting ½ cup

Marinade
Ginger, chopped 2 tbsp
Garlic, chopped ½ tbsp
Mint leaves, fresh 4 tbsp
Yogurt, hung, whisked 3½ tbsp (p. 5)
Pomegranate seeds, dried, crushed 1 tsp
Fenugreek leaves, dried, crushed 1 tsp
Red degi chilli powder 2 tsp
Cumin powder 2 tsp
Coriander powder 1 tsp
Dried mango powder 1 tsp
Garam masala powder 2 tsp
Black salt 1 tsp
Salt 2 tsp

- Remove the stems of the cauliflower florets, while keeping the florets whole.
- Parboil the florets in boiling salted water with the whole spices.
- Drain and set aside, till cool.

Marination

- Grind the ginger, garlic and mint leaves to make a smooth paste.
- Whisk the yogurt in a bowl with the ground paste and the remaining ingredients for the marinade.
- Rub the marinade all over the cauliflower.
- Cover and set aside to marinate in the refrigerator for 1 hour.

For the cauliflowers

- Remove the cauliflower from the refrigerator and bring to room temperature.
- Thread each cauliflower floret on to a thin, long metal skewer.
- Cook in a medium-hot tandoor or grill under a medium-hot gas or electric grill as described on pp. xiv–xv for 8–10 minutes.
- Baste with oil, turn the skewers and cook for 2–3 minutes longer.
- Slip the cauliflower off the skewers on to a serving platter.
- Serve hot with mint chutney (p. 12). Try it with wholewheat pita bread (p. 26) or tortillas (p. 28).

ARBI KEBAB

Makes 3–4

I never ate colocasia till I discovered this recipe. Truly a vegetarian delight.

Colocasia bulbs 500 gm

Marinade
Yogurt, hung, whisked 1 cup (p. 5)
Oil 1 tbsp
Carom seeds 1 tsp
Red chilli powder 1 tsp
Chaat masala powder 1 tsp
Salt 1 tsp

For the colocasia
Oil 4 tbsp
Onions, sliced 2
Coriander powder 1 tsp
Dried mango powder ½ tsp
Garam masala powder 1 tsp
Green cardamom powder 1 tsp
Salt 1 tsp
Lime juice 1 tsp
Lime, cut in wedges 2
Onion, sliced in rings 1

- Scrub the colocasia and drain.
- Put the colocasia in a pressure cooker with water to cover and pressure-cook for 10–15 minutes. Remove from heat and release the pressure under running cold water.
- Drain the colocasia and set aside, till cool.

- Peel and cut into rounds. Flatten the pieces slightly between your palms.

Marination
- Combine the ingredients for the marinade in a bowl and whisk well.
- Add the colocasia and mix well, to ensure that it is completely coated with the marinade.
- Cover and set aside to marinate in the refrigerator for 2–3 hours.

For the colocasia
- Arrange the colocasia on a lightly greased grill plate. Grill under a medium-hot grill for about 25 minutes or till the marinade dries up.
- Heat the oil in a frying pan. Add the onions and sauté on medium heat, till golden-brown.
- Add the spice powders, salt and grilled colocasia. Stir-fry for 4–5 minutes.
- Add lime juice and mix well.
- Transfer to a serving dish and serve hot with lime wedges and onion rings.

CORN KEBABS

Makes 3–4

A simple recipe especially loved by kids. My daughter Tanisha who likes cottage cheese and corn enjoys eating this kebab.

Corn kernels 500 gm
Green chillies, chopped fine 1 tbsp
Paneer 250 gm (p. 5)
Ginger-garlic paste 1 tsp
Lime juice 2 tsp
Coriander leaves, fresh, chopped fine 2 tbsp
Turmeric powder 1 tbsp
Red Kashmiri chilli powder 1 tsp
Cumin powder 1 tsp
Garam masala powder 1 tsp
Tandoori masala powder 1 tsp (p. 7)
Salt 2½ tsp
Oil, for basting 2 tbsp
Parsley, fresh, chopped 1 tsp
Tomato, cut into wedges 1

- Cook the corn kernels in boiling salted water, till tender. Drain and set aside.
- Mash the paneer in a bowl and mix in the corn kernels.
- Add the remaining ingredients for the kebabs and mix with your hands, till they blend well.
- Wet your hands and a few long, thick metal skewers.
- Roll the kebab mix into 12 balls and thread them on to the skewers. Shape the balls into small sausage-shaped kebabs along the length of the skewers, 1" apart.

For the kebabs
- Cook the kebabs in a medium-hot tandoor or grill under a medium-hot gas or electric grill as described on pp. xiv–xv for 7–8 minutes.

- Baste with oil, turn the skewers and grill again for another 4–5 minutes.
- Slip the kebabs off the skewers on to a serving platter. Sprinkle parsley on top and serve hot with tomato wedges and peanut chutney (p. 15).

RICE AND CORN KEBABS

Makes 3–4

This is a delicate kebab, easily made with the ingredients readily available in most kitchens.

Basmati rice 1 cup
Corn kernels, boiled ½ cup
Potato, boiled, mashed ⅓ cup
White vinegar 1 tsp
Green chillies, seeded, chopped fine 2
Coriander leaves, fresh, chopped fine 1 tbsp
Onion, chopped fine 1 tbsp
Ginger, chopped fine 1 tsp
Cornflour 1 tsp
Red chilli powder ½ tsp
Cumin powder ½ tsp
Green cardamom powder 1 tsp
White pepper, freshly ground ½ tsp
Salt 1½ tsp
Oil, for frying ½ cup
Chaat masala powder 1 tsp

- Wash the rice and soak it in water for 30 minutes.
- Drain the rice and boil in water, till cooked.
- Drain and grind the rice in a blender with the corn and mashed potato, to make a thick paste.
- Transfer to a bowl and add the remaining ingredients for the kebabs and mix till they blend well.
- Grease your hands lightly and divide the kebab mix into 6–8 equal portions. Shape into balls and flatten them slightly to form round patties.
- Heat the oil in a non-stick frying pan and shallow-fry the kebabs, till light golden-brown.

- Drain on kitchen paper.
- Sprinkle chaat masala powder on top and serve hot with Turkish lavash (p. 29) and mint chutney (p. 12) or mango chutney (p. 13).

JACKFRUIT KEBABS

Makes 6–8

When I was a kid I thought that jackfruit was meant to be eaten as a fruit. So whenever my mom bought it, I would order the butler to peel it and serve it to me chilled. Once he played a prank on me and actually peeled it and served it raw. I must have spent the whole day trying to convince my mom to terminate the butler's services with immediate effect. He then made this fabulous kebab for me to make amends.

Jackfruit, peeled, chopped 1 kg
Husked, split Bengal gram/chana dal 1 cup
Cloves 2
Green cardamoms 5
Black cardamoms 2
Turmeric powder 1 tsp
Salt 3 tsp
Green chillies, seeded, chopped fine 2
Chopped ginger 2 tsp
Coriander leaves, fresh, chopped fine 2 tbsp
Red chilli powder 1 tsp
Dried mango powder 1 tsp
Oil for frying 2 cups

- Bring a pan of water to boil on high heat. Add the jackfruit, dal, whole spices, turmeric powder and salt. Simmer on medium heat, till the jackfruit and dal are half cooked.
- Drain out the water and set aside till cool.
- Put the jackfruit and dal in a blender and mince them.
- Transfer to a bowl and add the remaining ingredients for the kebabs. Mix, till they blend well.
- Divide the kebab mix into 14 equal portions. Shape into balls and flatten them slightly to form round patties.

- Heat the oil in a frying pan and shallow-fry the kebabs, till golden-brown on both sides.
- Drain on kitchen paper.
- Serve hot with mango chutney (p. 13) and crisp naan (p. 33).

LOTUS STEM KEBABS

Makes 4

A rather unique dish inspired by Kashmiri cuisine. We had a Kashmiri festival in our restaurants recently and this was one of the most popular dishes on the menu.

Lotus stems 750 gm
Potatoes, medium-sized, boiled 2
Ginger, chopped fine 1½ tbsp
Green chillies, chopped fine 2 tbsp
Coriander leaves, fresh, chopped fine 2 tbsp
Red chilli powder 4 tsp
Cumin powder 1 tsp
Garam masala powder 2 tsp
Green cardamom powder ⅓ tsp
Nutmeg powder ⅓ tsp
Salt 2½ tsp
Breadcrumbs, fresh ½ cup
Oil for deep-frying
Tandoori masala powder ½ tsp (p. 7)
Coriander leaves, fresh, chopped 1 tsp
Lime, cut into wedges 1

- Scrub the lotus stems well. Peel and slice them. Boil in salted water, till tender. Drain and set aside, till cool.
- Grind the lotus stems in a food processor to make a fine mince.
- Add the boiled potatoes, ginger, green chillies and coriander leaves and grind again to blend.
- Transfer to a bowl and mix in the spice powders and salt.
- Add the breadcrumbs, a little at a time, to form a smooth paste that binds well.
- Wet your hands and divide the kebab mix into 14 equal

portions. Shape into balls and press them lightly to make round, flat, patties.
- Heat the oil in a frying pan. Fry the kebabs, till golden-brown on both sides.
- Drain on kitchen paper.
- Arrange the kebabs on a serving platter and sprinkle tandoori masala powder and coriander leaves on top. Serve hot with lime wedges, mango chutney (p. 13) and crisp naan (p. 33).

TANDOORI BHARWAN KHUMB

Makes 4–5

Mushroom caps stuffed with cottage cheese and grilled to perfection, are an all-time favourite. I usually eat them with Turkish lavash.

Mushrooms, large, kept whole 20

Filling
Paneer, grated 200 gm (p. 5)
Coriander leaves, fresh, chopped 3 tsp
Salt 1½ tsp

Marinade
Yogurt, hung, whisked ²/₃ cup (p. 5)
Oil 100 ml
Ginger-garlic paste 1 tbsp
Red chilli paste 1 tsp
Nigella seeds 2 tsp
Gram flour, roasted 2 tbsp
Mustard powder ½ tsp
Turmeric powder 1 tsp
Dried mango powder 1 tsp
Garam masala powder 2 tsp
Salt 2 tsp
Oil for basting

- Remove and discard the stems from the mushrooms.
- Wash the mushroom caps and blanch them in boiling salted water. Drain and put them into cold water immediately. When cool, drain and pat dry with paper towels.

Filling

- Combine the ingredients for the filling in a bowl and mix well.
- Scoop out the centre of the mushroom caps and stuff them with the filling.

Marinade

- Whisk the yogurt in another bowl with the remaining ingredients for the marinade.
- Gently lower the mushroom caps into the marinade and ensure they are completely coated.
- Cover and set aside to marinate in the refrigerator for about 1 hour.

For the mushrooms

- Remove the mushrooms from the refrigerator and bring to room temperature.
- Carefully thread the mushrooms on to long, thin metal skewers, 1" apart.
- Cook the mushrooms in a medium-hot tandoor; or grill under a medium-hot gas or electric grill as described on pp. xiv–xv for 6–7 minutes.
- Baste with oil, turn the skewers and grill again for another 3 minutes.
- Slip the mushrooms off the skewers on to a serving platter.
- Serve hot with mint chutney (p. 12) and Turkish lavash (p. 29).

POTATO KEBABS

TANDOORI ALOO TIKKA

Makes 3–4

This is a common dish served in almost all North Indian restaurants and is a bestseller.

Potatoes, medium-sized, cubed 2

Marinade
Yogurt, hung, whisked 2 tbsp (p. 5)
Oil ½ tbsp
Ginger-garlic paste 1 tbsp
Carom seeds 1 tsp
Gram flour 1 tsp
Red degi chilli powder 2 tsp
Cumin powder 1 tsp
Coriander powder 1 tsp
Dried mango powder 1 tsp
Garam masala powder 1 tsp
Black salt 1 tsp
Oil for frying ½ cup
Chaat masala powder 1 tsp

- Wash the potatoes and peel them. Cut them into 1½" cubes and parboil them in salted water. Drain and set aside till cool.

Marination
- Whisk the yogurt in a bowl with the remaining ingredients for the marinade.
- Add the potatoes and mix well, to ensure that they are completely coated with the marinade.
- Cover and set aside to marinate in the refrigerator for about 30 minutes.

For the tikka

- Remove the potatoes from the refrigerator and bring to room temperature.
- Thread the potatoes on to long, thin metal skewers, 1" apart.
- Cook the potatoes in a medium-hot tandoor or grill under a medium-hot gas or electric grill as described on pp. xiv–xv for 7–8 minutes.
- Remove and slip the potato pieces off the skewers.
- Heat the oil in a frying pan. Add the potatoes and stir-fry on high to medium heat, till crisp.
- Drain on kitchen paper.
- Sprinkle chaat masala powder on top and serve hot.

SESAME POTATO KEBABS

Makes 3–4

For this variation of the tandoori aloo tikka, which is famous in Moti Mahal, I have added a sesame-seed coating to give the popular recipe a twist. You will love it!

Potatoes, large 6
Salt 1 tsp
Sesame oil ½ cup

Coating
Cornflour 2 tbsp
Sesame seeds 1 tbsp
Salt ½ tsp

Filling
Sesame oil 1 tbsp
Butter, melted 2 tbsp
Cumin seeds 1 tsp
Turmeric powder 1 tsp
Red chilli powder 1 tsp
Coriander leaves, fresh, chopped 2 tbsp
Paneer, diced 1 cup (p. 5)
Potato, boiled, diced ½ cup
Raisins, seedless 1 tbsp
Salt 2 tsp
Sesame oil, for basting 2 tbsp

- Slice off the tops of the potatoes and reserve the slices.
- Scoop out the centre of the potatoes to make a hollow at least 1" deep.
- Wash the potatoes and the sliced tops and put them in a pan. Pour in just enough boiling water to cover and sprinkle in the salt. Blanch for 30 minutes.

- Remove from heat and drain. Pat the potato shells and sliced tops dry and set aside.

Coating
- Mix the cornflour in a bowl with just enough water to form a coating consistency.
- Roll the blanched potatoes in the cornflour mixture to coat completely.
- Spread the sesame seeds on a plate and roll the potatoes in the sesame seeds to coat completely.
- Heat the oil in a wok. Deep-fry the potatoes on low heat, till cooked through, but without changing colour.
- Remove and drain on kitchen paper.

Filling
- Heat the oil in a pan. Add the cumin seeds and sauté on medium heat for a few seconds.
- When the cumin seeds splutter, add the remaining ingredients for the filling. Sauté for 2–3 minutes.
- Remove from heat and empty on to a plate. Set aside, till cool.
- Divide the filling into 6 equal portions and stuff each potato with it.
- Cover with the reserved slices. Secure the cover with a toothpick.

For the kebabs
- Thread the potatoes on to a skewer, keeping them 1" inch apart.
- Cook the potatoes in a medium-hot tandoor as described on pp. xiv–xv for 3–5 minutes.
- Remove and baste with sesame oil. Cook for a further 2 minutes.
- Alternatively put the potatoes on a lightly greased grill plate. Put under a medium-hot grill for 5–6 minutes.
- Remove and baste with sesame oil. Grill for a further 2–3 minutes.

- Slip the potatoes off the skewers on to a serving platter. Remove and discard the toothpicks
- Serve hot with mint chutney (p. 12) or mango chutney (p. 13).

STUFFED TOMATO KEBABS

Makes 3

A rather simple recipe—easy to make and easy on the stomach. I love to eat this one with chilli garlic chutney and lavash bread.

Tomatoes, large, red, firm 6
Oil for basting
Chaat masala powder 2 tsp
Coriander leaves, fresh, chopped 2 tsp

Filling
Oil 1 tbsp
Cumin seeds 1 tsp
Ginger-garlic paste 1 tbsp
Paneer, cubed ½ cup (p. 5)
Green peas, shelled and boiled ½ cup
Potatoes, cubed and boiled ½ cup
Raisins, seedless 1 tbsp
Pineapple, canned, chopped 1 tsp
Coriander leaves, fresh, chopped 1 tbsp
Red chilli powder 1 tsp
Chaat masala powder 1 tsp
Salt 2 tsp

Marinade
Yogurt, hung, whisked 2½ tbsp (p. 5)
Egg, whisked 1
Asafoetida powder ¼ tsp dissolved in 1 tbsp water
Gram flour 7 tbsp
Red chilli powder 1 tsp
Salt 1 tsp

• Slice off the tops of the tomatoes and reserve the slices.

Scoop out the pulp and the seeds, carefully taking care not to break the shells.
• Wash the tomato shells and pat dry with paper towels.

Filling
• Heat the oil in a pan. Add the cumin seeds and sauté on medium heat, till they splutter.
• Add the ginger-garlic paste and stir for about 1 minute.
• Stir in the remaining ingredients for the filling and sauté for 3–4 minutes.
• Remove from heat and set aside, till cool.

Kebabs
• Stuff the tomatoes with the filling and cover with the reserved slices. Secure the cover with toothpicks.
• Set aside in the refrigerator for about 30 minutes.

Marination
• Combine the ingredients for the marinade in a bowl and whisk, till they blend well.
• Coat the tomatoes evenly with the marinade and set aside for about 1 hour.

To cook the kebabs
• Put the tomatoes on a lightly greased grill plate and grill under low heat for 3–5 minutes.
• Baste with oil and grill for 2–3 minutes longer.
• Transfer the tomatoes on to a serving platter. Remove and discard the toothpicks.
• Sprinkle chaat masala powder and coriander leaves on top and enjoy with Turkish lavash (p. 29).

YAM KEBABS

Makes 6–8

This is an interesting and unusual kebab recipe. I love yam as a vegetable, we often marinate it with salt, red chilli and vinegar and deep-fry it. It's a yummy snack and is appreciated at every party. Try this variation.

Yam 1½ kg
Green chillies, chopped fine 1 tsp
Ginger, chopped fine 1 tsp
Coriander leaves, fresh, chopped 1 tsp
Red chilli powder 1 tsp
Cumin powder 1 tsp
Chaat masala powder 1 tsp
White pepper powder 1 tsp
Salt 3½ tsp
Breadcrumbs, fresh ½ cup
Oil, for shallow-frying ¾ cup
Coriander leaves, fresh, chopped 1 tsp

- Peel the yam and wash thoroughly. Cut it into large chunks.
- Put the yam in a pan of salted water and bring to a boil. Reduce heat and simmer, till tender.
- Drain the yam thoroughly and grate it fine.
- Squeeze out all excess water from the yam and put it in a bowl.
- Add the remaining ingredients for the kebabs and mix, till they blend well.
- Wet your hands and divide the kebab mix into 8 equal portions. Shape into oval kebabs.
- Heat the oil in a frying pan.
- Shallow-fry the kebabs on medium heat, till crisp and golden-brown on all sides.

- Drain on kitchen paper.
- Arrange the kebabs on a serving platter and sprinkle
  coriander leaves on top. Serve hot with mint chutney (p. 12)
  and garlic flatbread (p. 31) or Turkish lavash (p. 29).

GARDEN VEGETABLE GRILL

Makes 2–3

This recipe needs no introduction; it's a simple, light, flavourful veggie dish that is an all-time favourite. The best part is that you may use any vegetables you have in your refrigerator.

Butternut 1, sliced into ¼" pieces
Aubergine, cut into ¼" slices 1
Red onion, cut in wedges 1
Red bell pepper, cut into 8 pieces 1
Green bell pepper, cut into 8 pieces 1
Mushroom caps, kept whole 4
Pineapple, fresh, cut into ½" cubes 8 pieces

Marinade
Olive oil 3 tbsp
Red wine vinegar 2 tbsp
Lime juice 2 tbsp
Basil leaves, fresh, chopped 1 tbsp
Parsley, fresh, chopped 1 tbsp
Garlic, minced 1 clove
Mustard powder 1 tbsp
Cumin powder 1 tsp
Black pepper, freshly ground ½ tsp
Salt 1 tsp
Parsley, fresh, chopped 1 tsp

- Cut the butternut and aubergines into ¼" slices.
- Cut the onion into quarters and separate the layers.
- Cut the bell peppers into 8 pieces.
- Keep the mushroom caps whole.

Marination
- Combine the ingredients for the marinade in a bowl and whisk well.

- Add the prepared vegetables and fruit and mix well, to ensure that they are completely coated with the marinade.
- Cover and set aside to marinate in the refrigerator for 2–3 hours.

For the kebabs
- Thread the vegetables and fruit alternately on to long, thin metal skewers.
- Place the skewers under a medium-hot gas or electric grill for 10–15 minutes.
- Brush with leftover marinade and grill again for 3–4 minutes, till the vegetables are tender and brown.
- Slip the vegetables and fruit off the skewers on to a serving platter. Sprinkle parsley on top and serve hot with steamed rice and chilli garlic chutney (p. 11).

TANDOORI SALAD

Makes 3–4

One of my all-time favourites on the Moti Mahal menu. Whenever I am having lunch at one of my restaurants this is a must for me as it is light and I love the delicate tandoori flavour of the marinated vegetables.

Tomatoes, medium-sized 2
Green bell pepper, medium-sized 2
Onions, medium-sized 2
Pineapple 100 gm
Paneer 100 gm (p. 5)
Oil, for basting 2 tsp
Chaat masala powder 2 tsp

Marinade
Yogurt, hung, whisked 1½ tbsp (p. 5)
Fenugreek leaves, dried 1 tsp
Carom seeds 1 tsp
Red degi chilli powder 1 tsp
Cumin powder 1 tsp
Garam masala powder 2 tsp
Black salt 1 tsp
Salt 2 tsp

- Cut the tomatoes into half and gently squeeze out the seeds.
- Cut all the vegetables, pineapple and paneer into large cubes.

Marination
- Whisk the yogurt in a bowl with the remaining ingredients for the marinade.
- Add the vegetables and mix well, to ensure that they are completely coated with the marinade.

- Cover and set aside to marinate in the refrigerator for 1 hour.

For the salad
- Remove the bowl from the refrigerator and bring to room temperature.
- Thread the vegetables, pineapple and paneer alternately on to metal skewers.
- Cook in a medium-hot tandoor or grill under a very hot gas or electric grill as described on pp. xiv–xv for about 5 minutes.
- Baste with oil, turn the skewers and grill again for another 2–3 minutes.
- Slip the vegetables off the skewers on to a serving platter.
- Sprinkle chaat masala powder on top and serve hot.

MIXED VEGETABLE AND VERMICELLI KEBABS

Makes 6

The vermicelli makes all the difference to this humble vegetable kebab. The crisply coated kebab, dipped in chilli garlic chutney, makes a perfect evening snack.

Carrots, roughly chopped 50 gm
French beans, roughly chopped 50 gm
Potato, small, roughly chopped 1
Mushrooms 30 gm
Coriander leaves, fresh, chopped 1 tbsp
Cumin powder 1 tsp
Garam masala powder 1 tsp
Chaat masala powder 1 tsp
Cashew nuts 1 tbsp
Raisins, seedless 1 tbsp
Salt 2 tsp
Breadcrumbs, fresh 1 cup
Vermicelli, crushed 25 gm
Oil for deep-frying

- Put all the vegetables in a pan with just enough water to cover. Cook on medium heat, till tender.
- Drain the vegetables thoroughly and grind to make a thick purée.
- Transfer to a bowl, add the remaining ingredients for the kebabs and mix till they blend well.
- Wet your hands and divide the kebab mix into 12 portions. Shape into balls.
- Spread the breadcrumbs and vermicelli in 2 separate plates.
- Roll the kebabs in the breadcrumbs and then in the vermicelli.

- Heat the oil in a kadhai or wok. Fry the kebabs, in batches, on medium heat, till golden brown.
- Drain on kitchen paper.
- Serve hot with chilli garlic chutney (p. 11).

HUNG YOGURT KEBABS

Makes 6–8

These soft and silky kebabs are a Moti Mahal bestseller.

Yogurt, hung, whisked 6 tbsp (p. 5)
Gram flour 2½ cups
Onions, chopped 3
Green chillies, chopped 4
Ginger, chopped 1½ tbsp
Coriander leaves, fresh, chopped 3 tbsp
Asafoetida powder ¼ tsp dissolved in 1 tbsp water
Cumin powder 1 tsp
Dried mango powder 1 tsp
Garam masala powder 2 tsp
Green cardamom powder ½ tsp
White pepper powder freshly ground 1 tsp
Salt 3 tsp
Oil, for frying ½ cup
Chaat masala powder 1 tsp
Onion, sliced in rings 1

- Combine the yogurt and gram flour in a bowl and mix, till they blend well.
- Press the mix through a strainer into a fresh bowl.
- Add the remaining ingredients for the kebabs and mix well.
- Knead gently, to form a soft dough.
- Cover and set aside in the refrigerator for 1 hour, to firm up.
- Grease your hands lightly and divide the kebab mix into 12 equal portions. Roll into balls and flatten them slightly to form round patties.
- Heat the oil in a frying pan. Fry the kebabs on medium heat on both sides, till golden-brown and crisp.
- Drain on kitchen paper.

- Transfer the kebabs to a serving platter. Sprinkle chaat masala powder and onion rings on top.
- Serve hot with mint chutney (p. 12).

COTTAGE CHEESE KEBABS
IN A SPICED GRAVY

MALAI PANEER TIKKA MASALA

Makes 2–3

Paneer is a delicacy, particularly for vegetarians, and any vegetarian will swear by this one. Succulent paneer cubes grilled, marinated with aromatic spices and fresh cream, yield a paneer tikka which melts in your mouth.

Paneer 250 gm (p. 5)
Tikka masala as made for fish tikka masala (pp. 195–6)
Oil, for basting 2 tbsp
Chaat masala powder 1 tsp

Marinade
Cashew nut and cheese paste ½ cup (p. 6)
Cream, fresh, whisked 2 tbsp
Ginger-garlic paste ½ tbsp
Coriander leaves, fresh, chopped 1 tbsp
Carom seeds 1 tsp
Dried mango powder 1 tsp
Green cardamom powder 1 tsp
White pepper powder 1½ tsp
Salt 1½ tsp

• Cut the paneer into 2" cubes.

Marination
• Combine the ingredients for the marinade in a bowl and whisk, till they blend well.
• Add the paneer pieces to the bowl.
• Mix gently to ensure that all the pieces are completely coated with the marinade.

- Cover and set aside to marinate in the refrigerator for about 30 minutes.

For the tikka
- Remove the paneer from the refrigerator and bring to room temperature.
- Thread the paneer on to long, thin metal skewers, 1" apart.
- Cook the tikka in a medium-hot tandoor or grill under a hot gas or electric grill as described on pp. xiv–xv for about 5 minutes.
- Baste with oil, turn the skewers and grill again for another 2–3 minutes.

Tikka masala
- Cook the tikka masala with the paneer in place of the fish (pp. 195–6).
- Serve hot sprinkled with chaat masala powder.

NOTE:
The tikka can also be served without the masala gravy.

SWEET AND SOUR COTTAGE
CHEESE KEBABS

KHATTA MEETHA PANEER
SHAHI TIKKA

Makes 2

When you are in a mood to eat something spicy and tangy, you may place your bets on this dish. A unique blend of cottage cheese and mango chutney, my mouth is watering even as I write this recipe.

Paneer 400 gm (p. 5)
Oil, for basting 1 tbsp
Coriander leaves, fresh, chopped 2 tbsp

Filling
Raw green mangoes, chopped 75 gm
Mint leaves, fresh, chopped 2–4
Curry leaves, fresh 2–4
Green chillies, chopped 2
Cumin powder 1 tsp
Salt 1 tsp

Marinade
Mango chutney 2 tsp (p. 13 or commercial)
Ginger-garlic paste 1 tbsp
Oil 1 tbsp
Salt 1½ tsp
Red chilli powder 1 tsp
Coriander powder ½ tsp
Chaat masala powder 1 tsp
Cornflour 1 tsp

• Cut the paneer into 1½" cubes. Make an incision in the centre of each piece without separating it.

Filling

- Combine the ingredients for the filling and grind to make a smooth paste.
- Reserve a quarter of the filling and stuff the paneer cubes with the remaining paste.

Marination

- Combine the reserved filling with the ingredients for the marinade in a bowl and whisk, till they blend well.
- Add the stuffed paneer pieces to the bowl.
- Mix gently to ensure that all the pieces are completely coated with the marinade.
- Cover and set aside to marinate in the refrigerator for 1 hour.

For the tikka

- Remove the paneer from the refrigerator and bring to room temperature.
- Thread the paneer on to long, thin metal skewers, 1" apart.
- Cook the kebabs in a medium-hot tandoor or grill under a very hot gas or electric grill as described on pp. xiv–xv for 7–8 minutes.
- Baste with oil, turn the skewers and grill again for another 4–5 minutes.
- Slip the kebabs off the skewers on to a serving platter. Sprinkle coriander leaves on top and serve hot with any chutney of your choice.

COTTAGE CHEESE AND PRUNE KEBABS

Makes 4–6

Another favourite fusion recipe. Prunes pair well with cottage cheese and leave a lightly sweet aftertaste.

Paneer, crumbled, made from 1 litre of milk (p. 5)
Oil for shallow-frying

Filling
Prunes, pitted, chopped fine 250 gm
Cheddar cheese, processed, grated 2 tbsp
Cashew nuts, crushed 1 tbsp
Green chillies, seeded, chopped 3
Coriander powder ½ tsp
Garam masala powder 1 tsp
Chaat masala powder 1 tsp
White pepper powder 1 tsp
Salt 2 tsp

Filling
- Combine the ingredients for the filling in a bowl. Mix well and set aside.

Kebabs
- Knead the paneer gently, till it forms a smooth dough.
- Wet your hands and divide the filling and paneer into 12 equal portions.
- Roll each portion of paneer into a ball and flatten it slightly between your palms.
- Put one portion of filling in the centre of a flattened ball and pull the edges up to cover the filling completely.
- Shape into a ball and flatten it slightly to form a round patty.
- Make all the kebabs in the same way.

- Put the kebabs in the refrigerator to firm up for at least 30 minutes.

To cook the kebabs
- Heat the oil in a non-stick frying pan. Shallow-fry the kebabs on medium heat, on both sides, till evenly cooked and crisp.
- Drain on kitchen paper.
- Transfer to a serving platter and serve hot with Norwegian flatbread (p. 27) and a cheese dip.

Glossary

English	Hindi
Allspice	Kebab cheeni
Almond	Badam
Aniseed	Chhoti saunf
Apricot	Khubani
Asafoetida	Hing
Aubergine/brinjal	Baingan
Bay leaf	Tej patta
Beef	Gai ka gosht
Bell pepper/capsicum	Shimla mirch
Bengal gram	
– Flour	Besan
– Husked, split	Chana dal
– Whole	Kala chana
Black cumin seeds	Kala jeera/shahi jeera
Black pepper	Kali mirch
Black salt	Kala namak
Bottle gourd	Ghia/lauki

English	Hindi
Bread	Double roti
Brinjal/aubergine	Baingan
Butter	Makkhan
– Clarified	Ghee
Capsicum	Shimla mirch
Cardamom	
– Black	Badi elaichi
– Green	Hari/chhoti elaichi
Carom seeds	Ajwain
Carrot	Gaajar
Cashew nut	Kaju
Cauliflower	Phoolgobhi
Chicken	Murgh
Chilli	Mirchi
– Dried red	Sookhi mirch
– Green	Hari mirch
– Red	Lal mirch
Cinnamon	Dalchini
Clove	Laung
Coconut milk	Nariyal ka doodh
Colocasia	Arbi
Coriander	
– Fresh	Hara dhania
– Whole seeds	Sabut dhania
Corn	Makkai
– Cob	Bhutta
– Meal	Makki ka atta
Cottage cheese	Paneer
Crab	Kekda
Cream	Malai

English	Hindi
Cumin seeds	Jeera
– Black cumin	Kala/shah jeera
Curd/yogurt	Dahi
Curry leaf	Kari patta
Duck	Batak
Egg	Anda
Fenugreek	
– Dry leaves	Kasuri methi
– Fresh leaves	Methi bhaaji
– Whole seeds	Methi dana
Fish	Machchi/machhli
Garlic	Lassun
Gingelly/ sesame seed oil	Til ka tael
Ginger	
– Dry	Saunth
– Fresh	Adrak
Green peas	Mattar
Groundnut	Mungphali
Honey	Madh/shahad
Jackfruit	Kathal
Jaggery	Gur
Kidney beans	Rajma
Lettuce	Salad ke patté
Lime	Limbu/nimbu
Lobster	Barra jhinga
Mace	Javitri
Mango	Aam
– Dried powder	Amchur
Marrow/bottle gourd	Ghia/lauki

English	Hindi
Milk	Doodh
Mince	Keema
Mint	Pudina
Mushroom	Dhingri/ khumb
Mustard	
– Oil	Sarson ka tael
– Seeds	Sarson/rai
– Yellow	Peeli sarson
Mutton	Gosht
Nigella	Kalaunji
Nutmeg	Jaiphal
Oil	Tael
– Hydrogenated vegetable oil	Vanaspati
Onion	Pyaaz
Papaya	Papeeta
– Unripe	Kaccha papeeta
Peanut	Mungphali
Peppercorn	Kali mirch
Pickle	Achaar
Pineapple	Annanas
Pistachio nuts	Pista
Pomegranate	Anar
– Dry seeds	Anardana
Pomfret	Chhamna/paplet
Poppy seeds	Khus-khus
Pork	Suvar ka gosht
Potato	Alu
Prawn	Jhinga
Raisin	Munakka
– seedless	Kishmish

English	Hindi
Rice	Chaval
Rock salt	Lohori namak
Rose water	Gulabjal
Saffron	Kesar/zafran
Salt	Namak
Sesame	
– Oil	Til ka tael
– Seeds	Til
Shrimp	Jhinga
Sodium bicarbonate	Meetha soda
Spinach	Palak
Sugar	Cheeni/shakkar
Tamarind	Imli
Tomato	Tamatar
Turmeric	Haldi
Vermicelli	Sevian
Vinegar	Sirka
Walnut	Akhrot
White salmon	Rawas
Yam	Zimikand
Yogurt	Dahi

Index of Recipes

BASIC RECIPES
Brown Onion Paste   4
Cashew nut and Cheese Paste   6
Garlic Paste   3
Ginger Paste   3
Hung Yogurt   5
Onion Paste   3
Paneer (Cottage Cheese)   5
Tomato Purée   4

CHUTNEYS
Aam ki Chutney (Mango Chutney)   13
Coriander Chutney   11
Lasun-Mirch Chutney (Chilli Garlic Chutney)   11
Pudina Chutney (Mint Chutney)   12
Peanut Chutney   15
Til aur Tamatar ki Chutney (Sesame Tomato Chutney)   14

FLATBREADS
Pita Bread   24
Wholewheat Pita Bread Cooked on the Stove Top   26
Tortillas   28
Rosemary Flatbread   32
Moroccan Flatbread   30
Norwegian Flatbread   27

Turkish Lavash   29
Italian Flatbread   36
Garlic Flatbread   31
Makhan Roti (Butter Flatbread)   34
Indian Naan   33

MEAT KEBABS

Beef
Bihari Kebabs (Sliced Beef Kebabs)   108
Kebab Halabi (Syrian Meat Loaf)   106
Kebab Torsh (Grilled Beef in a Pomegranate Marinade)   110

Chops
Minted Mutton Chops   97
Mutton Chops   101
Tabak Maas (Kashmiri Chops)   95
Tundey Kebab (Batter-Fried Mutton Chops)   99

Mutton
Ali Nazik Kebabi (Minced Mutton with Aubergine Purée)   63
Bahcivan Kebabi (Gardener's Kebabs)   86
Beyti Kebab (Minced Mutton Kebabs in Pita Wraps)   61
Braised Mutton Shanks in Aubergine Wraps   103
Bugu Kebabi (Steamed Kebabs)   84
Burrah Kebab (North West Frontier Mutton Kebabs)   69
Chapli Kebab (Spicy Minced Mutton Patties)   39
Chelow Kebab (Iranian Minced Mutton Kebabs)   57
Chislic (Tangy Meat Kebabs)   82
Digi Kebab (Baked Mutton Kebabs)   45
Fenugreek Mutton Kebabs   67
Galouti Kebab (Melt-in-the-Mouth Kebabs)   46
Kebab-e-Barg (Sliced Mutton Kebabs)   91
Kebab-e-Kubideh (Iranian Minced Mutton Kebabs)   59
Kafta (Arabian Hamburger)   56
Kakori Kebab (Smoked Mutton Patties)   43
Kashmiri Shammi Kebab (Minced Mutton Patties)   41
Lucknowi Pasanda Kebab (Sliced Mutton Kebabs)   89
Minted Mutton Chops   97
Paprika Kebabs   281
Peshawari Boti Kebab (Mutton Kebabs from Peshawar)   71

Rajasthani Boti Kebab (Mutton Kebabs from Rajasthan)   65
Satay (South East Asian Barbecue)   93
Seekh Kebab (Minced Mutton Kebabs)   50
Seekh Kebab Gilafi (Minced Mutton Kebabs in a Crisp Coating)   52
Shikhampuri Kebab (Stuffed Mince Patties)   48
Suya or Tsire Kebab (West African Meat Kebabs)   77
Tabak Maas (Kashmiri Chops)   95
Testi Kebab (Clay-Pot Kebabs)   87
Tundey Kebab (Batter-Fried Mutton Chops)   99
Mutton Chops   101
Mutton Tikka Masala (Mutton Kebabs in a Spiced Gravy)   73
Yogurtlu Kebab (Mutton Kebabs with Yogurt)   79

Mixed Meats
Ćevapčići or Čevapi (Bosnian Mixed Mince Kebabs)   114
Sheftalia (Greek Sausages)   112
Shrimp and Steak Kebabs   223

Pork
Ćevapčići or Čevapi (Bosnian Mixed Mince Kebabs)   114
Sheftalia (Greek Sausages)   112

POULTRY KEBABS
Chicken
Afghani Chicken   176
Banno Kebab (Chicken Kebabs in a Crisp Coating)   134
Bharwan Tangri Kebab (Stuffed Chicken Drumsticks)   178
Chicken and Gram Kebabs   139
Chicken Rum Kebabs   153
Chicken Tikka   193
Dum ka Murgh Kebab (Slow-Cooked Chicken Kebabs)   145
Garden Green Chicken Tikka   141
Garlic Chicken Kebabs   130
Ginger Chicken Kebabs   137
Greek Chicken Kebabs with Feta Mint Sauce   167
Grilled Chicken, Red Onion and Mint Kebabs with Greek Salad   171
Honey Chicken Kebabs   157
Hyderabadi Chicken Kebabs   126
Joojeh Kebab (Iranian Chicken Kebabs)   155
Kandahari Chicken Kebabs   128

Minted Chicken Kebabs   143
Moroccan Chicken Kebabs   159
Murgh Badam Pasanda (Almond Chicken)   173
Murgh Gilafi Kebab (Chicken Kebabs in a Crisp Coating)   116
Nigella Chicken Kebabs   147
Peanut-Flavoured Chicken Kebabs   118
Pesto Chicken Kebabs   161
Pistachio Chicken Kebabs   163
Rajasthani Murgh Burrah (Chicken Kebabs)   122
Red Curry Chicken Kebabs   169
Saffron Chicken Kebabs   124
Shish Touk (Lebanese Chicken Kebabs)   151
Tandoori Chicken   181
Teriyaki Chicken Kebabs   165
Thai Chicken Kebabs   149
Turkish Chicken Shish Kebab   132

Duck
Tandoori Duck   183

Quail
Tandoori Quail   185

RAITAS AND SALADS
Chukundar aur Anar Raita (Beetroot and Pomegranate Relish)   21
Greek Salad   21
Irani Raita (Cucumber and Yogurt Relish)   19
Jeera Raita (Cumin and Yogurt Relish)   19
Moroccan Couscous Salad   22
Palak Raita (Spinach and Yogurt Relish)   20

SAUCES
Hot Chilli Sauce   16
Hot Satay Peanut Sauce   16
Teriyaki Sauce   17

SEAFOOD KEBABS
Fish
Amritsari Fish   187

Fenugreek Fish Kebabs   199
Kebab-e-Ozunborun (Rock Salmon Kebabs)   205
Machchi Tikka (Fish Kebabs)   193
Machchi Tikka Masala (Fish Kebabs in a Spiced Gravy)   195
Pudina Machhli Tikka (Minted Fish Kebabs)   201
Salmon Basil Tikka   203
Tamarind Fish Tikka   197
Tandoori Pomfret   189
Tandoori Salmon   191

Shellfish
Coconut Prawn Kebabs   213
Crab and Prawn Kebabs   221
Garlic Chilli Prawn Kebabs   211
Prawn Kebabs with Mango Chilli Salsa   215
Prawn Kebabs with Pesto Sauce   219
Tandoori Lobster   225
Tandoori Prawns   207
Tangy Thai Prawn Kebabs   217
Thai Chilli Tandoori Prawns   209

SPICE BLENDS
Aromatic Spice Masala Powder   6
Garam Masala Powder   6
Tandoori Masala Powder   7
Zhoug (Middle Eastern Spice Blend)   8

VEGETABLE KEBABS
Arbi Kebabs (Grilled Colocasia)   240
Bengal Gram Kebabs   234
Bottle Gourd Kebabs   236
Corn Kebabs   242
Asparagus Kebabs   227
Cottage Cheese and Prune Kebabs   273
Garden Vegetable Grill   261
Hung Yogurt Kebabs   267
Jackfruit Kebabs   246
Khatta Meetha Paneer Shahi Tikka   271
Lotus Stem Kebabs   248

Malai Paneer Tikka Masala (Cottage Cheese Kebabs in a Spiced
Gravy)   269
Minted Tandoori Cauliflower   238
Mixed Vegetable and Vermicelli Kebabs   265
Red Kidney Bean Kebabs   230
Rice and Corn Kebabs   244
Sesame Potato Kebabs   254
Stuffed Tomato Kebabs   257
Tamarind Paneer Tikka   198
Tandoori Aloo Tikka (Potato Kebabs)   252
Tandoori Bharwan Khumb (Stuffed Tandoori Mushrooms)   250
Tandoori Salad   263
White Bean Kebabs   232
Yam Kebabs   259

Monish Gujral, a graduate from Delhi University, studied hotel management at the Institute of Hotel Management, Catering and Nutrition, Pusa, Delhi, before joining his illustrious grandfather, Kundan Lal Gujral, at his restaurant, Moti Mahal. Not only has Monish kept his grandfather's legend alive, he has expanded the brand and launched the Moti Mahal Delux® Tandoori Trail chain of restaurants, with pan India and international operations, spread over a hundred franchises. Monish's first cookbook was a bestseller in several countries and was chosen as the finalist for the 10th Gourmand World Cookbook Awards, 2004. *On the Butter Chicken Trail*, his second cookbook, won the Gourmand World Best Easy Recipe Cookbook 2009.

~